Welcome to

A POCKET Style Manual

EIGHTH EDITION, APA VERSION

Faster and more reliable than a Google search, *A Pocket Style Manual* covers everything you need for college writing in APA style. You can turn to it for help with finding, evaluating, integrating, and citing sources — as well as for advice on revising sentences for clarity, grammar, and punctuation. The following reference aids will help you find everything you need to be a successful college writer in any course.

- **The brief and detailed contents** inside the front and back covers allow you to quickly spot the help you need.

- **The index** at the back of the book includes plain-language entries like "*I* vs. *me*" to point to common problems like pronoun case.

- **A wealth of resources for writing in APA style** are provided, including models for in-text APA citations and reference list entries, as well as annotated sample pages from 11 student papers.

- **The glossaries** on pages 229–246 offer useful definitions and help with commonly confused or misused words such as *affect/effect*.

If your instructor has assigned a Hacker Handbooks media product, even more help is at your fingertips:

- **Nearly 300 exercises** help you improve your writing and effectively work with sources.

- **50 model papers** in five documentation styles provide guidance in writing and formatting your work in any course.

- **33 LearningCurve quizzes** offer gamelike sentence-level practice and let you track your progress.

EIGHTH EDITION

A POCKET
Style Manual

APA VERSION

Diana Hacker

Nancy Sommers
Harvard University

Contributing Author
Rick A. Matthews
Carthage College

bedford/st.martin's
Macmillan Learning
Boston | New York

For Bedford/St. Martin's

Vice President, Editorial, Macmillan Learning Humanities: Edwin Hill
Executive Program Director for English: Leasa Burton
Executive Program Manager: Stacey Purviance
Marketing Manager: Vivian Garcia
Director of Content Development: Jane Knetzger
Senior Executive Editor for Handbooks: Michelle Clark
Development Editor: Will Stonefield
Senior Media Editor: Barbara G. Flanagan
Associate Editor: Melissa Rostek
Content Project Manager: Lidia MacDonald-Carr
Senior Workflow Project Supervisor: Joe Ford
Production Supervisor: Robin Besofsky
Senior Media Project Manager: Allison Hart
Manager of Publishing Services: Andrea Cava
Project Management: Lumina Datamatics, Inc.
Composition: Lumina Datamatics, Inc.
Photo Permissions Editor: Angela Boehler
Text Permissions Manager: Kalina Ingham
Director of Design, Content Management: Diana Blume
Cover Design: William Boardman
Printing and Binding: RR Donnelley

Printed in China.

1   2   3   4   5   6   23   22   21   20   19   18

For information, write: Bedford/St. Martin's, 75 Arlington Street, Boston, MA 02116

ISBN 978-1-319-05743-5

Acknowledgments

Acknowledgments and copyrights appear on the same page as the text and art selections they cover; these acknowledgments and copyrights constitute an extension of the copyright page.

Writing Papers in APA Style

1 Writing college papers in APA style

In most of your college courses, it's likely you will be asked to complete one or more writing assignments. Besides composition courses, a wide variety of college courses require writing. Many different types of writing—essays, laboratory reports, memos, and treatment plans, for example—are assigned in many types of courses, such as psychology, sociology, business, and nursing. Instructors in these courses typically ask their students to write in the style recommended by the American Psychological Association (APA).

APA style is a set of rules and guidelines for writers in the social sciences (psychology, sociology, criminal justice, anthropology, political science) and in business, education, and nursing. When you are assigned a paper for a particular class, you should think of that assignment as an opportunity to join a discourse community—a group of thinkers and writers in a field who share interests, ideas, and ways of communicating with one another. When you adhere to APA style, you satisfy your readers' expectations and allow them to focus attention on the substance of your writing without unnecessary distractions.

APA style may be used for many types of writing, or *genres*. The following are the most common types of papers assigned in courses in which APA style is required:

- research paper: literature review
- research paper: original empirical research
- laboratory report
- analytical essay
- annotated bibliography
- administrative report
- case study
- clinical paper
- professional memo
- reflective essay
- social issue paper

Sections 1a–1k describe the requirements of these types of papers. Section 10 gives details about the typical parts of APA-style papers. And section 12 contains excerpts from several papers written in APA style.

1a Research paper: Literature review

The ideas, theories, and findings of scholars published in academic journals or books contribute to what researchers call "the literature" on a topic.

A common research assignment in undergraduate classes is a literature review. When you write a literature review, you formulate a research question and collect sources that have been written about your question. You summarize and synthesize the sources, indicating how they relate to one another and what insights they contribute to your question. You can also suggest ways that future research might add clarity to the conversation.

For instance, suppose you settled on the research question "What is the relationship between poverty rates and property crime rates in urban communities?" In answering this question, you might compare data from the U.S. Census Bureau about the incidence of poverty in a particular group of cities and data from the Uniform Crime Reports about the incidence of property crime in those cities to see if a statistically significant relationship exists.

A review of the literature may be incorporated in other types of papers, especially empirical research papers and laboratory reports. In an empirical research paper, the literature review section is typically more extensive and longer than in a laboratory report. (See also 1b and 1c.)

1b Research paper: Original empirical research

An empirical research paper is a report on an original study that you design and data that you collect, perhaps from interviews, experiments, surveys, or observations in the field. Such data are called *primary data*. A research paper may also include *secondary data* — results from studies by other researchers that are relevant to the design of your study and the analysis of your data.

In an empirical research paper, you state a research question or a hypothesis, briefly describe the work of others on the topic, present the methods you used to but most involve a deep analysis of a relatively narrow subject.

Some case studies require primary data—data that you collect. For an education class, you might study the effectiveness of particular classroom management techniques. Your study might involve observing a classroom in which those techniques are used and drawing conclusions based on your observations.

Or a case study might involve a detailed description and analysis of an event, such as the federal or state response to a natural disaster. A case study can also be used to study a single organization as an example of a larger issue—for example, you might study the 2016 scandal involving Wells Fargo's fake bank accounts as an example of corporate mismanagement.

1h Clinical paper

Clinical papers are most often used by practitioners in the health professions to share information about clients. A clinical paper usually provides an overview of a client's background and symptoms, reviews the relevant literature on the client's condition, and then provides details and recommendations about the course of treatment as well as actual and expected results.

1i Professional memo

Memos are widely used by employees of a business or members of another organization to communicate with one another. Memos may identify a problem or concern within the organization, inform others about a policy or procedure, assign tasks to people, or solve a problem (or all of these things at once). Memos are often sent via email.

Memos may cover a wide range of subjects and may be any length. A short memo might simply contain a task for the members of a committee. A longer memo might contain a proposal with data or ideas that are not your own.

When writing a memo, make sure that the content, language, and tone are appropriate for the intended audience (see also 2b and 2c). Memos usually provide ongoing documentation for a project and may be helpful to those doing similar projects in the future, so your audience may be broader than the initial recipients of the memo.

1j Reflective essay

A reflective essay is personal writing, usually used to explore how an experience shaped your understanding of an issue or a topic in your discipline. For example, a reflective essay about your student-teaching experience may include a description of how your perspective on a learning theory changed once you were teaching your own class.

1k Social issue paper

The social issue paper is a common assignment in college writing courses. This genre requires you to take a position on a contemporary social issue—what social scientists call a policy debate. For example, one possible topic for a social issue paper is whether the government should tax junk food at a higher rate than healthy food.

A typical assignment asks you to identify a social issue, articulate a research question, find scholarly sources about the issue, and then come to your own conclusion based on the sources you have read. Your goal is to clearly articulate your position (or thesis) and marshal persuasive evidence to support your point of view, while also fairly expressing other perspectives on the issue.

2 Understanding APA conventions

Writers and researchers in the social sciences and in business, education, and nursing follow APA standards, or *conventions*, a set of agreed-upon rules. You may be asked to use these conventions to guide your own practices as you search for and evaluate sources, draft your writing, and acknowledge the contributions of others. The APA conventions that you will be expected to follow in your writing are detailed in this section.

2a Privileging current sources

While recognizing that knowledge is based on ideas and findings that have emerged over time, APA style values the currency of research. *When* a person wrote a book or an article or conducted research can be as important as *what* that person wrote or researched. The dates of the research you cite in your paper indicate to your readers that you are building your own work on the most recent work of others and that you understand the connection between your work and the work that has come before.

At the same time, you will likely find older sources that are relevant to your research question. While there is nothing wrong with citing older sources, you should make clear in your paper how those findings connect to more recent research in the field. One way to determine the validity of previous research is to look for more recent articles that have cited older work. When analyzing the results of the more recent research, check whether the work supports the original findings. Doing so will help you determine whether the older research is still valid and, if so, how it aligns with your work and that of contemporary researchers.

The author's name and the publication date are given both in citations of sources within a paper and in the reference list at the end of the paper, as shown below. (For more details about the use of direct quotations, see section 9. For more information on citing and documenting sources in APA style, see sections 13–15.)

IN-TEXT CITATION

Gawande (2009) noted that technology "has added yet another element of complexity to the systems we depend on and given us entirely new kinds of failure to contend with" (p. 184).

REFERENCE LIST ENTRY

Gawande, A. (2009). *The checklist manifesto: How to get things right.* New York, NY: Metropolitan Books.

2b Using appropriate tone and language

APA style calls for writing that is direct, clear, concise, engaging, objective, and formal. Researchers often prefer the active voice, which is more direct and concise, to the passive voice (see also 17).

PASSIVE VOICE (LENGTHY, INDIRECT)

Support for faster female response times was found in several studies (Barber, 2010; Lee, 2009; Sumner, 2011).

The idea that social meaning is largely constructed through the interactions people have with one another has been emphasized by symbolic-interaction theorists.

ACTIVE VOICE (CONCISE, DIRECT)

Several studies (Barber, 2010; Lee, 2009; Sumner, 2011) supported faster female response times.

Symbolic-interaction theorists have emphasized that social meaning is largely constructed through the interactions people have with one another.

In general, use nouns and third-person pronouns (see 27c) whenever possible. But sometimes for clarity and to avoid the passive voice, the first person (*I* or *we*) is appropriate, especially in the abstract and the method section in research papers and laboratory reports when you are describing your own procedures. Also, in reflective essays and research involving observation in the field, the first person is appropriate to describe your own experiences or to relate your experiences to a larger issue or larger body of work.

THIRD PERSON, PASSIVE VOICE

Participants were selected with a random number generator.

The children's behavior toward their peers was observed both in the classroom and on the playground.

FIRST PERSON, ACTIVE VOICE

I selected the participants with a random number generator.

We observed the children's behavior toward their peers both in the classroom and on the playground.

NOTE: When writing in the first person, use the plural *we* only if you have coauthors; use *I* if you are the only author.

APA style requires the past tense (*explained*) or present perfect tense (*have written*) for describing the work of others or for your own results. (See 9b.) You may use the present tense to describe the applications or effects of your results (*the data indicate*).

2c Avoiding stereotypes, bias, and offensive language

Your writing must be respectful and free of stereotypical, biased, or other offensive language. Be especially careful when describing or labeling people in terms of their race, age, disability, gender, or sexual orientation.

Labels can become dated, and it is important to recognize when their continued use is not acceptable. When naming groups of people, choose labels that the groups currently use to describe themselves. For example, *Negro* is not an acceptable label for African Americans; some people prefer the term *Native American* to *Indian*, and even better is to use the name of the specific group (*Lakota, Sioux*).

Be as specific as possible when describing age groups (*women aged 24 to 30 years,* not *young women* or *twentysomethings*), and avoid terms such as *elderly* or *senior*, which can be vague and can also carry a negative connotation.

Do not identify a person by a condition or disability; refer to the person first, the condition or disability second. Use *men with epilepsy* rather than *epileptics* or *epileptic men*. The term *client* is preferred to *patient* in many fields.

Use gender-neutral language (*firefighter, legislator* instead of *fireman, congressman*). When possible, use plural pronouns rather than the singular *he, him, his* or the wordy and noninclusive *he or she, him or her, his or her*. (See also 24d on avoiding sexist language and 27a on indefinite pronouns.) Currently acceptable terms for describing sexual orientation are *lesbian, gay,* and *bisexual* rather than *homosexual*.

It's a good idea to check with your instructor or someone else in the discipline about the currently acceptable terms for describing and labeling people.

2d Understanding intellectual property

The term *intellectual property* refers to published works, ideas, and images that have been created by an individual or a group. When you use the intellectual property of others in your own work—by quoting, summarizing, or paraphrasing—you must give credit to the source of the information. Failure to do so is a form of academic dishonesty called *plagiarism*. (See also section 8.)

Besides summarizing, paraphrasing, or quoting another's work without proper citation, it is considered plagiarism to submit someone else's work as your own (such as by purchasing a paper or hiring someone to write a paper for you).

Consistent and proper use of the APA system of citation—in the text of the paper and in the reference list at the end of the paper—will ensure that you do not misrepresent the intellectual property of someone else as your own. (See sections 13–15 for details on the APA system of citation.)

2e Collecting and reporting data

For some types of papers, you may collect and report data yourself—from surveys you administer, from experiments you conduct, from audio or video interviews you record, from observations you make in the field, and so on. APA conventions require you to collect and report data in an ethical manner.

In collecting your data, be careful not to ignore groups of research participants whose responses you think may prove contrary to your research question. In reporting your findings, you must not ignore or downplay results that contradict other results or results you expected to find. If your research involves human participants, you must preserve confidentiality. And you must not falsify data or report results in a misleading way, such as by manipulating images or creating graphs with only partial data.

A standard in the social sciences is that research must be replicable—that is, other researchers must be able to use the information provided in your paper to conduct a study of their own to try to reproduce your results. If you do not collect data objectively and honestly or if you report data in a misleading way, others will not be able to come close to replicating your findings, even if they use the same method.

2f Protecting research participants

Ethics codes in the social sciences are intended to protect research participants from physical or emotional harm and to prevent falsifying data, misrepresenting research findings, and plagiarizing. Whenever you plan to collect data through interviews, surveys, experiments, or observation, determine whether your research project needs the review and approval of your school's institutional review board (IRB).

An IRB requires that participation in research be voluntary, that the research participants grant informed consent, and that they not be harmed (either emotionally or physically). Participants should be able to end their participation at any time without penalty. Researchers must observe confidentiality and must conduct their research with integrity and ensure that it has academic value.

Some kinds of research are exempt from IRB approval. If you analyze data that have been collected and published by someone else, those data generally are exempt from IRB review. In addition, most large data sets used in undergraduate research courses — such as the General Social Survey and the Uniform Crime Reports — are exempt, as are published data from studies conducted by organizations, commissions, government agencies, and the like.

If you are unsure whether your project needs IRB approval, ask your instructor.

3 Posing questions to start a paper

Most college assignments begin with a question worth exploring. The question might be posed in the wording of the assignment, or you might be required to come up with your own question. For a research paper, you might search for answers in books, in articles, and on websites; for a laboratory report, your answers might come from an experiment you design; for a business memo, you might conduct a customer survey. Your answers should guide your interpretation and lead to reasoned conclusions supported with valid and well-documented evidence.

Within the guidelines of your assignment, begin by asking questions that you are interested in exploring, that you believe will interest your audience, and that will contribute to an ongoing debate or to existing knowledge in the field.

For any type of assignment, you should make sure that your questions are narrow (not too broad), challenging (not too bland), and grounded (not too speculative).

3a Choosing a narrow question

If your initial question is too broad for the length you were assigned, look for ways to restrict your focus. Here, for example, is how two students narrowed their initial questions.

TOO BROAD	NARROWER
What are the hazards of fad diets?	What are the hazards of low-carbohydrate diets?
What are the benefits of stricter auto emission standards?	How will stricter auto emission standards create new, more competitive auto industry jobs?

3b Choosing a challenging question

Your paper will be more interesting to both you and your audience if you base it on an intellectually challenging line of inquiry. Try to draft questions that provoke thought or, if your purpose is to take a position, engage readers in a debate.

TOO BLAND	CHALLENGING
What is obsessive-compulsive disorder?	Why is obsessive-compulsive disorder so difficult to treat?
What were client S.R.'s symptoms?	How did the combined course of drug therapy and physical therapy reduce client S.R.'s symptoms?

You may need to address a bland question in the course of answering a more challenging one, but it would be a mistake to use the bland question as the focus for the whole paper.

3c Choosing a grounded question

Finally, you will want to make sure that your question is grounded, not too speculative. Although speculative questions—such as those that address moral issues or beliefs—are worth asking and may receive attention in some papers, they are inappropriate central questions. In most papers, the central point should be grounded in facts.

TOO SPECULATIVE	GROUNDED
Is it wrong to share pornographic personal photos by cell phone?	What role should the U.S. government play in regulating mobile content?
Do students have the right to listen to music during class?	What effect does listening to music while studying have on adolescents' test performance?

4 Finding appropriate sources

Whatever your topic and your question, some sources will prove more useful than others. For example, if your question addresses whether a particular public policy has been effective, you might want to look at scholarly articles, books, reference works, and government documents. If the policy is the subject of current debate, you might also want to read magazines and newspaper articles, websites, and documents from organizations that try to influence public policy (such as think tanks).

4a Locating reference works

For some topics, you may want to begin your search by consulting general or specialized reference works. General reference works include encyclopedias, almanacs, atlases, and biographical references. Many specialized reference works are available: *Encyclopedia of Bioethics, The Encyclopedia of Social Work, Almanac of American Politics,* and *The Historical and Cultural Atlas of African Americans*, to name a few. Reference works can help you learn about a topic, but you will need to consult more in-depth sources as you write.

The reference librarians at your school are trained to assist you in finding sources and can be helpful as you conduct your research. You should take advantage of their expertise if you have questions about how to evaluate sources. They can also help you as you refine your research question or topic.

4b Locating articles

Libraries subscribe to a variety of databases (sometimes called *periodical* or *article databases*) that give students access to articles and other materials without charge. Older works that have not been digitized will not be available in databases, so you may need to consult a print index as well.

What databases offer Your library's databases can lead you to articles in newspapers, magazines, and scholarly or technical journals. General databases cover several subject areas; subject-specific databases cover one subject area in depth. Your library might subscribe to some of the following databases.

GENERAL DATABASES

Academic Search Premier, a database that indexes popular and scholarly journals

Expanded Academic ASAP, a database that indexes the contents of magazines, newspapers, and scholarly journals

JSTOR, a full-text archive of scholarly journals from many disciplines

LexisNexis, a set of databases with particular emphasis on news and business, legal, and political topics

ProQuest, a database of periodical articles

SUBJECT-SPECIFIC DATABASES

Business Source Premier, an index of business abstracts and titles

Criminal Justice Abstracts, a database for criminal justice research

ERIC, an education database

Health Source: Nursing/Academic Edition, a database for nursing topics

PsycINFO, a database of psychology research

PubMed, a database with abstracts of medical studies

Many databases include the full text of at least some articles; others list only citations or citations with short summaries called *abstracts*. When the full text is not available, a citation will give you enough information to track down an article.

How to search a database   To find articles on your topic in a database, start by searching with keywords, terms related to the information you need. If the first keyword you try results in no matches, try some synonyms. If your keyword search results in too many matches, narrow it by using one of the strategies in the chart on the next page.

You can also narrow your topic by looking for repeated subjects within your search results. For example, a search on the death penalty will yield many results, but you might notice when you read through the titles of the results that multiple articles address the constitutionality of the death penalty and many other articles discuss prisoners who were wrongly convicted and put to death—in other words, two specific topics within the broader subject of the death penalty. Looking for these kinds of patterns can help you narrow your research topic.

Finally, some databases allow you to search for peer-reviewed articles. Using this feature will limit your search results to articles that have been through the rigorous peer-review process, meaning that other experts working in the field read and approved the articles before they were published. Limiting your search results to peer-reviewed articles is one way to make sure that your sources contain accurate information.

4c Locating books

The books your library owns, along with other resources, are listed in its catalog. You can search the catalog by author, title, or subject.

If your search calls up too few results, try different keywords or search for books on broader topics. If your search gives you too many results, try the strategies in the chart on the next page.

Use a book's call number to find the book on the shelf. When you're retrieving the book, take time to scan other books nearby, since they are likely to cover the same topic.

> ### Refining keyword searches in databases and search engines
>
> Although command terms and characters vary among databases and online search engines, some of the most common functions are listed here.
>
> - Use quotation marks around words that are part of a phrase: "gateway drug."
> - Use AND to connect words that must appear in a document: hyperactivity AND children. Some search engines require a plus sign instead: hyperactivity+children.
> - Use NOT in front of words that must not appear in a document: Persian Gulf NOT war. Some search engines require a minus sign (hyphen) instead: Persian Gulf-war.
> - Use OR if only one of the terms must appear in a document: "mountain lion" OR cougar.
> - Use an asterisk as a substitute for letters that might vary: "marine biolog*" (to find *marine biology* or *marine biologist*).
> - Use parentheses to group a search expression and combine it with another: (standard OR student OR test*) AND reform.
>
> **NOTE:** Many search engines and databases offer an advanced search option for refining your search with filters for phrases that should or should not appear, date restrictions, and so on.

4d Locating other sources online

You can find a variety of reliable resources using online tools beyond those offered by your library. For example, government agencies post information on their websites, and the sites of many organizations are filled with information about current issues. Museums and libraries often post digital versions of primary sources, such as photographs, political speeches, and classic texts.

Although the Internet can be a rich source of information, it lacks quality control. Be sure to evaluate online sources with special care (see 5c).

This section describes the following Internet resources: search engines, digital archives, government sites, news sites, blogs, and wikis.

Search engines   When using a search engine, such as Google Scholar, focus your search as narrowly as possible. You can sharpen your search by using the tips listed in the chart on the previous page or by using a search engine's advanced search form. In Google Scholar, each article also includes a list of related articles, which can help you find additional sources on your topic.

Digital archives   Archives like the following can help you find primary resources such as the text of books, poems, speeches, and historically significant documents; photographs; and political cartoons.

> *American Memory*: memory.loc.gov
>
> *Avalon Project*: avalon.law.yale.edu
>
> *Eurodocs*: eudocs.lib.byu.edu
>
> *Google Books*: books.google.com
>
> *Google Scholar*: scholar.google.com
>
> *Online Books Page*: onlinebooks.library.upenn.edu

Government sites   For current topics, government sites can prove useful. Many government agencies at every level provide online information. Government-maintained sites include resources such as facts and statistics, legal texts, government reports, and searchable reference databases. Here are just a few government sites:

> *Census Bureau*: www.census.gov
>
> *FedStats*: fedstats.sites.usa.gov
>
> *Government Publishing Office*: www.gpo.gov/fdsys
>
> *National Criminal Justice Reference Service*:
> www.ncjrs.gov
>
> *United Nations*: www.un.org

News sites   Many news organizations offer up-to-date information online. Some sites require registration and charge fees for some articles. (Find out if your library subscribes to news sites that you can access at no charge.) The following news sites offer many free resources:

> *BBC*: www.bbc.co.uk
>
> *Google News*: news.google.com
>
> *New York Times*: www.nytimes.com
>
> *Reuters*: www.reuters.com

Blogs A blog is a site that contains text or multimedia entries usually created and maintained by one person, with comments contributed by readers. Though some blogs are personal or devoted to partisan politics, many journalists and academics maintain blogs that cover topics of interest to researchers. The following websites can lead you to a wide range of blogs:

> *Academic Blog Portal*: academicblogs.org
>
> *Science Blogs*: scienceblogs.com
>
> *Technorati*: technorati.com

Wikis A wiki is a collaborative website with many contributors and with content that may change frequently. Wikipedia, a collaborative online encyclopedia, is one of the most frequently consulted wikis.

In general, Wikipedia may be helpful if you're checking for something that is common knowledge or looking for current information about a topic in contemporary culture. (For a discussion of common knowledge, see 8a.) However, many scholars do not consider Wikipedia and wikis in general to be appropriate sources for college research. Authorship is not limited to experts; articles may be written or changed by anyone. When possible, locate and cite a more reliable source for any useful information you find in a wiki.

5 Evaluating sources

You can often locate dozens or even hundreds of potential sources for your topic—far more than you will have time to read. Your challenge will be to determine what kinds of sources you need and to find a reasonable number of high-quality sources.

Later, once you have decided on sources worth consulting, your challenge will be to read them with an open mind and a critical eye.

5a Selecting sources

Determining how sources contribute to your writing
How you plan to use sources affects how you evaluate

them. Sources can contribute to your paper in various ways. You can use them to

- provide background information or context for your topic
- explain terms or concepts that your readers might not understand
- provide evidence for your main idea
- lend authority to your discussion
- offer counterevidence and alternative interpretations

For examples of how student writers use sources for a variety of purposes, see section 9.

Scanning search results The box in section 4d shows how to refine your searches. This section explains how to scan through the results for the most useful and reliable sources.

Databases Most article databases (see 4b) provide at least the following information to help you decide if a source is relevant, current, scholarly, and of a suitable length.

> Title and brief description (How relevant?)
>
> Date (How current?)
>
> Name of periodical (How scholarly?)
>
> Length (How extensive in coverage?)

Book catalogs A book's title and date of publication are often your first clues about whether the book is worth consulting. If a title looks interesting, you can click on it for further information.

Search engines Because anyone can publish a website, legitimate sources and unreliable sources live side by side online. Look for the following clues about the probable relevance, currency, and reliability of a site—but be aware that the clues are by no means foolproof.

> Title, keywords, and lead-in text (How relevant?)
>
> Date (How current?)
>
> Indications of the site's sponsor or purpose (How reliable?)
>
> The URL, especially the domain name extension, such as .com, .edu, .gov, or .org (How relevant? How reliable?)

Determining if a source is scholarly

Many college assignments require you to use scholarly sources. Written by experts for a knowledgeable audience, these sources often go into more depth than books and articles written for a general audience. To determine if a source is scholarly, look for the following:

- Formal language and presentation
- Authors with academic or scientific credentials
- Footnotes or a bibliography documenting the works cited by the author in the source
- Original research and interpretation (rather than a summary of other people's work)
- Quotations from and analysis of primary sources
- A description of research methods or a review of related research
- An abstract (a short summary of the article)

If you are searching in an online database, another way to make sure that a source is scholarly is to filter your search results by peer-reviewed articles. All peer-reviewed articles are scholarly and have been thoroughly fact-checked by other experts in the field.

See the next page for a sample scholarly source and a sample popular source.

5b Reading with an open mind and a critical eye

As you begin reading the sources you have chosen, keep an open mind. Do not let your personal beliefs prevent you from considering new ideas and opposing viewpoints. Your question—not a snap judgment about the question—should guide your reading.

When you read critically, you are not necessarily judging an author's work harshly; you are simply examining its assumptions, assessing its evidence, and weighing its conclusions. (See the checklist on evaluating sources in section 5c.)

5c Assessing online sources with special care

Sources on the Internet can provide valuable information, but verifying their credibility may take time. Here's one way to think about it: If you find an online

Common features of a scholarly source

1. Formal presentation with abstract and research methods
2. Includes review of previous research studies
3. Reports original research
4. Includes references
5. Multiple authors with academic credentials

FIRST PAGE OF ARTICLE

Cyberbullying: Using Virtual Scenarios to Educate and Raise Awareness

Vivian H. Wright, Joy J. Burnham, Christopher T. Inman, and Heather N. Ogorchock **5**

1

Abstract

This study examined cyberbullying in three distinct phases to facilitate a multifaceted understanding of cyberbullying. The phases included (a) a quantitative survey, (b) a qualitative focus group, and (c) development of educational scenarios/simulations (within the Second Life virtual environment). Phases I and II were based on adolescent feedback about cyberbullying from Phases I and II of this study. In all three phases, adolescent reactions to cyberbullying were examined and reported to raise awareness and to educate others about cyberbullying. Results from scenario development indicate that simulations created in a virtual environment are engaging and have the potential to be powerful tools in helping schools address problems such as cyberbullying education and prevention. (Keywords: cyberbullying, virtual worlds, Second Life, teacher education, counselor education)

Introduction

Cyberbullying has gained attention and recognition in recent years (Beale & Hall, 2007; Carney, 2008; Casey-Canon, Hayward, & Gowen, 2001; Kowalski & Limber, 2007; Li, 2007; Shariff, 2005). The increased interest and awareness of cyberbullying relates to such factors as the national media attention after several publicized cyberbullying tragedies (Maag, 2007; Stelter, 2008; Zifcak, 2006), the attenuation of communication [...] and computer network [...] technology use among youth, presently there remai [...] cyberbullying and its possibi [...] lescents. Because cyberbully [...] systems (i.e., home, school, a [...] "school professionals" (Li, 2007, p. 1778), and mental health providers must not only be made aware of cyberbullying and its consequences, but must also have access to ways to deal with this growing concern.

Two years ago, cyberbullying was considered to be a "new territory" for exploration (Li, 2007, p. 1778) because there was limited information about bullying through "electronic means" (Li, p. 1780). In contrast, today studies on cyberbullying, including some descriptions of the worst cyberbullying incidences (Maag, 2007; Stelter, 2008; Zifcak, 2006), are becoming more prevalent (Beale & Hall, 2007; Carney, 2008; Kowalski & Limber, 2007; Li, 2007). At this time, there is a need to raise awareness about the effects of cyberbullying and to create educational opportunities to serve multiple audiences (i.e., teachers, teacher educators, school administrators, school counselors, mental health professionals, students, parents) in the quest to identify and hopefully prevent cyberbullying in the future. Consequently, to facilitate a multifaceted understanding of

cyberbullying, this study sought to examine cyberbullying through three phases: (a) a quantitative survey, (b) a qualitative focus group, and (c) development of the educational scenarios/simulations (i.e., using virtual world avatars similar to those used in Linden Lab's (1993) Second Life (SL; http://secondlife.com) based on adolescent feedback from Phases I and II of this study. Adolescent reactions to cyberbullying in all three phases of this study were examined and reported with two aims in mind: (a) to raise awareness of cyberbullying, and (b) to educate others about cyberbullying.

Defining Cyberbullying

Cyberbullying has been described as a traumatic experience that can lead to physical, cognitive, emotional, and social consequences (Carney, 2008; Casey-Canon et al., 2001; Patchin & Hinduja, 2006). Cyberbullying has been defined as "bullying through the e-mail, instant messaging, in a chat room, on a website, or though digital messages or images sent to a cell phone" (Kowalski & Limber, 2007, p. 822). There are numerous methods to engage in cyberbullying, including e-mail, instant messaging, online gaming, chat rooms, and text messaging (Beale & Hall, 2007; Li, 2007). In addition, cyberbullying appears in different forms than traditional bullying. For example, Beale & Hall (2007), Mason (2007), and Willard (2008) found that at least seven different types of cyberbullying exist, including:

* [...] information
* Exclusion: excluding someone purposefully

2 Research suggests that cyberbullying has distinct gender and age differences. According to the literature, girls are more likely to be online and to cyberbully (Beale & Hall, 2007; Kowalski & Limber, 2007; Li, 2006, 2007). This finding is "opposite of what happens off-line," where boys are more likely to bully than girls (Beale & Hall, p. 8). Age also appears to be a factor in cyberbullying. Cyberbullying increases in the elementary years, peaks during the middle school years, and declines in the high school years (Beale & Hall). Based on the literature, cyberbullying is a growing concern among middle school-aged children (Beale & Hall; Hinduja & Parchin, 2008; Kowalski & Limber, 2007; Li, 2007; Pellegrini & Bartini, 2000; Smith, Mahdavi, Carvalho, & Tippett, 2006; Williams & Guerra, 2007). Of the middle school grades, 6th grade students are usually the

Volume 26/ Number 1 Fall 2009   Journal of Computing in Teacher Education   35
Copyright © 2009 ISTE (International Society for Technology in Education), 800.336.5191 (U.S. & Canada) or 541.302.3777 (Int'l), iste@iste.org, www.iste.org

© 2009 ISTE (International Society for Technology in Education).

EXCERPTS FROM OTHER PAGES

3
Table 2: Percentage of Students Who Experienced Cyberbullying through Various Methods

	E-mail	Facebook	MySpace	Cell Phone	Online Video	Chat Rooms
Victim	35.3%	11.8%	52.9%	50%	14.7%	11.8%
Bully	17.6%	0%	70.6%	47.1%	11.8%	5.9%

4
References

Bainbridge, W. S. (2007, July). The scientific research potential of virtual worlds. *Science, 317,* 472–476.

Beale, A., & Hall, K. (2007, September/October). Cyberbullying: [...]

5 *Vivian H. Wright is an associate professor of instructional technology at the University of Alabama. In addition to teaching in the graduate program, Dr. Wright works with teacher educators on innovative ways to infuse technology in the curriculum to*

Wright, V. H., Burnham, J. J., Inman, C.T., & Ogorchock, H. N. (2009). Cyberbullying: Using virtual scenarios to educate and raise awareness. *Journal of Computing in Teacher Education, 26*(1), 35–42.

Common features of a popular source

1 Eye-catching title
2 Written by a staff reporter, not an expert
3 Presents anecdotes about the topic
4 Sources are named, but no formal reference list appears
5 Presents a summary of research but no original research

ONLINE ARTICLE

CNN Health

Home TV & Video U.S. World Politics Justice Entertainment Tech Health Living Travel Opinion iReport Money Sports

Part of complete coverage on
Bullying   SPECIAL REPORT: BULLYING

When bullying goes high-tech 1

by **Elizabeth Landau**, CNN 2
updated 2:12 PM EDT, Mon April 15, 2013

STORY HIGHLIGHTS
• As many as 25% of teenagers have experienced cyberbullying
• Among young people, it's rare that an online bully will be a total stranger
• Researchers are working on apps and algorithms to detect and report bullying online

(CNN) -- Brandon Turley didn't have friends in sixth grade. He 3 would often eat alone at lunch, having recently switched to his school without knowing anyone.

While browsing MySpace one day, he saw that someone from school had posted a bulletin -- a message visible to multiple people -- declaring that Turley was a "fag." Students he had never even spoken with wrote on it, too, saying they agreed.

EXCERPT FROM A LATER SECTION

A pervasive problem
As many as 25% of teenagers have experienced cyberbullying at some point, said Justin W. Patchin, who studies the 4 phenomenon at the University of Wisconsin-Eau Claire. He and colleagues have conducted formal surveys of 15,000 middle and high school students throughout the United States, and found that about 10% of teens have been victims of cyberbullying in 5 the last 30 days.

> **Evaluating all sources**
>
> **Checking for signs of bias**
>
> - Does the author or publisher endorse political or religious views that could affect objectivity?
> - Is the author or publisher associated with a special-interest group, such as Greenpeace or the National Rifle Association, that might present a narrow view of an issue?
> - Does the author's language show signs of bias?
>
> **Assessing an argument**
>
> - What is the author's central claim or thesis?
> - How does the author support this claim—with relevant and sufficient evidence or with anecdotes or emotional examples?
> - Are statistics accurate and used fairly? Does the author explain where the statistics come from?
> - Are any of the author's assumptions questionable?
> - Does the author treat opposing arguments fairly and refute them persuasively?

article that has not been peer-reviewed and you do not know who the author is, then you have to do the work of checking the author's credentials and determining whether the information is reliable. By contrast, if you find a peer-reviewed scholarly article, that work has already been done for you by experts in the field.

Even sites that appear to be professional and fair-minded may contain questionable information. Before using an online source in your paper, make sure you know who created the material and for what purpose. The chart on the next page provides a checklist for evaluating online sources.

6 Managing information; avoiding plagiarism

Whether you decide to record information about your sources on paper or on your computer—or both—you will need methods for managing that information: maintaining a working bibliography, keeping track of source materials, and taking notes without plagiarizing

Evaluating online sources

Authorship

- Is there an author? You may need to do some clicking and scrolling to find the author's name. Check the home page or an "about this site" link.
- Can you tell whether the author is knowledgeable and credible? If the author's qualifications aren't listed on the site, look for links to the author's home page, which may provide evidence of his or her expertise.
- Does the author cite sources? Do those sources appear reliable?

Sponsorship

- Who, if anyone, sponsors the site? The sponsor of a site is often named and described on the home page.
- What does the URL tell you? The domain name extension often indicates the type of group hosting the site: commercial (.com), educational (.edu), nonprofit (.org), governmental (.gov), military (.mil), or network (.net). URLs may also indicate a country of origin: .uk (United Kingdom) or .jp (Japan), for instance. The domain name extension .com.co often leads to fake news sites and other misleading information.

Purpose and audience

- Why was the site created: To argue a position? To sell a product? To inform readers?
- Who is the site's intended audience?

Currency

- How current is the site? Check for the date of publication or the latest update.
- How current are the site's links? If many of the links no longer work, the site may be outdated for your purposes.

your sources. (For more on avoiding plagiarism, see section 8.)

6a Maintaining a working bibliography

Keep a record of any sources you decide to consult. This record, called a *working bibliography*, will help you compile the list of sources at the end of your paper. (For more details about documenting sources, see part 3.)

Once you have created a working bibliography, you can annotate it. Writing several brief sentences summarizing the key points of a source in your own words will help you identify how the source relates to your argument and to your other sources. Clarifying your sources' ideas at this stage will help you separate them from your own ideas and avoid unintentional plagiarism later.

SAMPLE ANNOTATED BIBLIOGRAPHY ENTRY

International Monetary Fund, Western Hemisphere Department. **1**

(2010). *United States: 2010 article IV consultation*
(Country Report No. 10/249). Retrieved from http://
www.imf.org/external/pubs/ft/scr/2010/cr10249.pdf

The International Monetary Fund publishes an
annual report on each member country's economic status
within the global economy. The report outlines the **2**
country's efforts in creating international and domestic
economic stability while offering recommendations to
address the country's economic challenges. The 2010 **3**
report on the United States provides important statistics
showing the United States' decrease in imports and
exports during the current economic crisis and the effect
of this contracting trade on the international community.
The report also lists specific challenges that face the
United States as it continues to recover from the crisis.
The report helps me put recent U.S. macroeconomic **4**
policy trends, as well as several of my other sources,
in context; it also gives me a basis for evaluating the
effects of these policies in both the short and the long
term. I can use the report to draw conclusions about the **5**
effectiveness of these largely Keynesian policies as well
as predict future policy revisions.

1   Use APA reference list format for each entry.
2   Summarize the source.
3   Annotations should be three to seven sentences long.
4   Evaluate the source for relevance and describe how it
relates to other sources you might use in the paper.
5   Evaluate how the source might contribute to your paper.

6b Keeping track of source materials

Save a copy of each source either digitally or in print. Many databases will allow you to email, save, or print citations, abstracts, or full texts of articles, and you can easily download, copy, print, or take screenshots of information from websites.

Working with saved files or printouts—as opposed to relying on memory or hastily written notes—lets you highlight key passages and make notes in the margins of the source as you read. You also reduce the chances of unintentional plagiarism because you will be able to compare your use of a source in your paper with the actual source, not just with your notes.

NOTE: It's especially important to keep print or digital copies of sources that you find online. Such sources may change or even become inaccessible over time. Make sure that your copy includes the site's URL and your date of access.

6c Avoiding unintentional plagiarism as you take notes

When you take notes, be careful to identify borrowed words and phrases as quotations. Even if you half-copy the author's sentences—either by mixing the author's phrases with your own without using quotation marks or by plugging your synonyms into the author's sentence structure—you are committing plagiarism, a serious academic offense.

Summarizing and paraphrasing ideas and quoting exact language are three ways of taking notes. Learning how to summarize and paraphrase without plagiarizing takes practice. One way to develop these skills is to avoid looking at the original passage as you write your summary or paraphrase. This method may help you avoid accidentally copying words, phrases, or sentence structure from the original passage. Be sure you understand the author's meaning so that the ideas from the source take shape in both your own words and your own presentation, distinct from the original text.

Whenever you include a direct quotation, a summary, or a paraphrase in your notes, be sure to include exact page references. For all three types of notes, you will need the page numbers later if you use the

Integrating and citing sources to avoid plagiarism

Source text

Our language is constantly changing. Like the Mississippi, it keeps forging new channels and abandoning old ones, picking up debris, depositing unwanted silt, and frequently bursting its banks. In every generation there are people who deplore changes in the language and many who wish to stop its flow. But if our language stopped changing it would mean that American society had ceased to be dynamic, innovative, pulsing with life—that the great river had frozen up.

—Robert MacNeil and William Cran,
Do You Speak American? (2005), p. 1

NOTE: For details on integrating sources, see section 9. For citing sources in the text of the paper, see section 13.

If you are using an exact sentence from a source, with no changes . . .	→	. . . put quotation marks around the sentence. Use a signal phrase and include a page number in parentheses.

MacNeil and Cran (2005) have written, "Our language is constantly changing" (p. 1).

If you are using a few exact words from the source but not an entire sentence . . .	→	. . . put quotation marks around the exact words that you have used from the source. Use a signal phrase and include a page number in parentheses.

Some people, according to MacNeil and Cran (2005), "deplore changes in the language" (p. 1).

If you are using near-exact words from the source but changing some word forms (*I* to *she*, *walk* to *walked*) or adding words to clarify and make the quotation flow with your own text . . .	→	. . . put quotation marks around the quoted words and put brackets around the changes you have introduced. Include a signal phrase and follow the quotation with the page number in parentheses.

MacNeil and Cran (2005) compared the English language to the Mississippi River, which "forg[es] new channels and abandon[s] old ones" (p. 1).

MacNeil and Cran (2005) have written, "In every generation there are people who deplore changes in the [English] language and many who wish to stop its flow" (p. 1).

If you are paraphrasing or summarizing the source, using the author's ideas but not any of the author's exact words . . .	→	. . . introduce the ideas with a signal phrase and put the page number at the end of your sentence. Do not use quotation marks. (See 8c.)

MacNeil and Cran (2005) argued that changes in the English language are natural and that they represent cultural progress (p. 1).

If you have used the source's sentence structure but substituted a few synonyms for the author's words . . .	→	STOP! This is a form of plagiarism even if you use a signal phrase and a page number. Change your sentence by using one of the techniques given in this chart or in section 9.

PLAGIARIZED
MacNeil and Cran (2005) claimed that, like a river, English creates new waterways and discards old ones (p. 1).

INTEGRATED AND CITED CORRECTLY
MacNeil and Cran (2005) claimed, "Like the Mississippi, [English] keeps forging new channels and abandoning old ones" (p. 1).

information in your paper. (See the chart above for further advice about avoiding plagiarism.)

7   Supporting a thesis

For assignments that call for research—literature reviews, empirical research papers, analytical essays, and annotated bibliographies, among others—you will form a research question that will lead to a thesis statement or a statement of your central idea (see section 3 on posing questions). You will usually present your thesis in the introduction, the first few paragraphs of the paper. The rest of the paper will draw on the sources you use to support your thesis.

You face three main challenges when writing a paper that draws on sources: (1) supporting a thesis, (2) citing your sources and avoiding plagiarism (see section 8), and (3) integrating quotations and other source material (see section 9).

7a Forming a working thesis

Once you have read a variety of sources and considered your issue from different perspectives, you are ready to form a working thesis—a one-sentence (or occasionally two-sentence) statement of your central idea. The thesis expresses your informed, reasoned judgment, not your opinion. Usually your thesis will appear at the end of the first paragraph.

As you learn more about your subject, your ideas may change, and your working thesis will evolve too. You can revise your working thesis as you draft.

In your research paper, your thesis will answer the central question that you pose. Here are some examples.

RESEARCH QUESTION

Is medication the right treatment for the escalating problem of childhood obesity?

POSSIBLE THESIS

Understanding the limitations of medical treatments for children highlights the complexity of the childhood obesity problem in the United States and underscores the need for physicians, advocacy groups, and policymakers to search for other solutions.

RESEARCH QUESTION

How can a business improve employee motivation?

POSSIBLE THESIS

Setting clear expectations, sharing information in a timely fashion, and publicly offering appreciation to specific employees can help align individual motivation with corporate goals.

RESEARCH QUESTION

Why are boys diagnosed with ADHD more often than girls?

POSSIBLE THESIS

Recent studies have suggested that ADHD is diagnosed more often in boys than in girls because of personality differences between boys and girls as well as gender bias in referring adults, but an overlooked cause is that ADHD often coexists with other behavior disorders that exaggerate or mask gender differences.

Each of these thesis statements expresses a view based on the sources the writer consulted or the original research the writer conducted. The writers will need to show readers how their evidence supports their thesis.

7b Testing your thesis

When drafting and revising a thesis statement, make sure that it's suitable for your writing purpose and that you can successfully develop it with the sources available to you. Keeping the following guidelines in mind will help you develop a successful thesis statement.

- A thesis should take a position that needs to be explained and supported. It should not be a fact or a description.

- A thesis should be your answer to a question, your solution to a problem, or your position on a topic or debate. It should not simply present a question, problem, or topic.

- A thesis should match the scope of the assignment. If your thesis is too broad to be covered adequately, explore a subtopic of your original topic. If your thesis is so narrow that you don't have much to say, find out what debates surround your topic and take a position.

- A thesis should be sharply focused. Avoid vague words such as *interesting* or *good*. Use concrete language and make sure your thesis lets readers know what you plan to discuss.

- A thesis should stand up to the "So what?" question. Ask yourself why readers should be interested in your paper and care about your thesis. If your thesis matters to you, your readers are more likely to find your ideas engaging.

7c Organizing your ideas

APA encourages the use of headings to help readers follow the organization of a paper. For empirical research papers and laboratory reports, the major headings are "Method," "Results," and "Discussion." In other papers, the headings will vary, depending on the type of paper and the topic. (See also 10i.)

7d Using sources to inform and support your argument

Sources can play several different roles as you develop your points.

Providing background information or context Use facts and statistics to support generalizations or to establish the importance of your topic.

Explaining terms or concepts Explain words, phrases, or ideas that might be unfamiliar to your readers. Quoting or paraphrasing a source can help you define terms and concepts in accessible language.

Supporting your claims Back up your claims and conclusions with facts, data, examples, and other evidence from your research.

Lending authority to your argument Expert opinion can give weight to your argument or discussion. But don't rely on experts to make your points for you. Express your ideas in your own words and cite authorities in the field to support your position.

Anticipating and countering other interpretations Do not ignore sources that seem contrary to your thesis or that offer interpretations different from your own. Instead, use them to give voice to opposing ideas and interpretations before you counter them.

8 Avoiding plagiarism

A paper that relies on research is a collaboration between you and your sources. To be fair and ethical, you must acknowledge your debt to the writers of those sources. When you acknowledge your sources, you avoid plagiarism, a serious academic offense.

Three different acts are considered plagiarism: (1) failing to cite quotations and borrowed ideas, (2) failing to enclose borrowed language in quotation marks, and (3) failing to put summaries and paraphrases in your own words. (See also 2d.)

8a Citing quotations and borrowed ideas

When you cite sources, you give credit to writers from whom you've borrowed words or ideas. You also let your readers know where your information comes from, so that they can evaluate the original source.

You must cite anything you borrow from a source, including direct quotations, statistics and other specific facts, visuals such as graphs and diagrams, and any ideas you present in a summary or a paraphrase.

The only exception is common knowledge—information that your readers may know or could easily locate in general sources. For example, most general encyclopedias will tell readers that Sigmund Freud wrote *The Interpretation of Dreams* and that chimpanzees can learn American Sign Language. When you have seen certain information repeatedly in your reading, you don't need to cite a source for it. However, when information has appeared in only a few sources, when it is highly specific (as with statistics or data from government agencies), or when it is controversial, you should cite the source.

APA recommends an author-date style of citations. Here, briefly, is how the author-date system usually works. See sections 13–15 for a detailed discussion of variations.

1. The source is introduced by a signal phrase that includes the last name of the author followed by the date of publication in parentheses.
2. The material being cited is followed by a page number in parentheses.
3. At the end of the paper, an alphabetized list of references gives publication information for the source.

IN-TEXT CITATION

Bell (2010) reported that students engaged in student-centered learning performed better on both project-based assessments and standardized tests (pp. 39–40).

ENTRY IN THE LIST OF REFERENCES

Bell, S. (2010). Project-based learning for the 21st century: Skills for the future. *The Clearing House, 83*(2), 39–43.

8b Enclosing borrowed language in quotation marks

To show that you are using a source's exact phrases or sentences, you must enclose them in quotation marks. To omit the quotation marks is to claim—falsely—that the language is your own. Such an omission is plagiarism even if you have cited the source.

ORIGINAL SOURCE

> Student-centered learning, or student centeredness, is a model which puts the student in the center of the learning process.
>
> —Z. Çubukçu, "Teachers' Evaluation of Student-Centered Learning Environments" (2012), p. 50

PLAGIARISM

According to Çubukçu (2012), student-centered learning is a model which puts the student in the center of the learning process (p. 50).

BORROWED LANGUAGE IN QUOTATION MARKS

According to Çubukçu (2012), "student-centered learning . . . is a model which puts the student in the center of the learning process" (p. 50).

NOTE: Quotation marks are not used when quoted sentences are set off from the text by indenting (see 9a).

8c Putting summaries and paraphrases in your own words

A summary condenses information from a source; a paraphrase conveys information in about the same number of words as in the original source. When you summarize or paraphrase, you must name the source and restate the source's meaning in your own words. You commit plagiarism if you half-copy, or patchwrite, the author's sentences—either by mixing the author's phrases with your own without using quotation marks or by plugging synonyms into the author's sentence structure. The following paraphrases are plagiarism—even

though the source is cited—because their language and
structure are too close to those of the source.

ORIGINAL SOURCE

> Student-centered teaching focuses on the student.
> Decision-making, organization and content are
> determined for most by taking individual students'
> needs and interests into consideration. Student-
> centered teaching provides opportunities to develop
> students' skills of transferring knowledge to other
> situations, triggering retention, and adapting a high
> motivation for learning.
>   —Z. Çubukçu, "Teachers' Evaluation
>   of Student-Centered Learning
>   Environments" (2012), p. 52

PLAGIARISM: UNACCEPTABLE BORROWING OF PHRASES

According to Çubukçu (2012), student-centered teaching takes
into account the needs and interests of each student, making it
possible to foster students' skills of transferring knowledge to new
situations and triggering retention (p. 52).

PLAGIARISM: UNACCEPTABLE BORROWING OF STRUCTURE

According to Çubukçu (2012), this new model of teaching centers
on the student. The material and flow of the course are chosen by
considering the students' individual requirements. Student-centered
teaching gives a chance for students to develop useful, transferable
skills, ensuring they'll remember material and stay motivated (p. 52).

To avoid plagiarizing an author's language, don't
look at the source while you are summarizing or paraphrasing. After you've presented the author's ideas in
your own words, return to the source and check that
you haven't used the author's language or sentence
structure or misrepresented the author's ideas.

There is more than one correct way to paraphrase.
Below are three different acceptable paraphrases of the
same passage. All three paraphrases avoid plagiarism
by citing the original source and by using different
language and sentence structure than the source.

ACCEPTABLE PARAPHRASES

1. Çubukçu's (2012) research documents the numerous benefits
of student-centered teaching in putting the student at the center

of teaching and learning. When students are given the option of deciding what they learn and how they learn, they are motivated to apply their learning to new settings and to retain the content of their learning (p. 52).

2. According to Çubukçu (2012), students perform better in student-centered environments—that is, environments where they have greater control over what they learn and how they learn. Students in such environments are more likely to retain the information they learn and to apply that information outside the classroom (p. 52).

3. Çubukçu (2012) identifies significant advantages to learning in a student-centered classroom. Students who decide what they learn about and how they learn it experience increased motivation and greater ability to apply what they have learned. They also remember more of what they learn (p. 52).

NOTE: APA recommends using a page number after a summary or a paraphrase to help readers locate the passage in the source.

8d Avoiding self-plagiarism

You should respond to each assignment with original work. Submitting the same work (or portions of it) for two different assignments—even if the assignments are years apart or for different instructors—is usually considered self-plagiarism. Each assignment is an opportunity to explore new ideas or gain new perspective. If a new assignment benefits from writing or research you completed for an older assignment, you should cite your earlier work using proper APA style. If you are unsure about what constitutes self-plagiarism for a particular assignment or paper, you should talk to your instructor.

9 Integrating sources

Quotations, summaries, paraphrases, and facts will help you develop your ideas, but they cannot speak for you. You can use several strategies to integrate information from sources into your paper while maintaining your own voice.

9a Using quotations appropriately

Limiting your use of quotations   In your writing, keep the emphasis on your own words. Do not quote excessively. It is not always necessary to quote full sentences from a source. Often you can integrate words or phrases from a source into your own sentence structure.

Citing federal data, *The New York Times* reported a 30% drop in "people entering teacher preparation programs" between 2010 and 2014 (Rich, 2015).

Using the ellipsis mark   To condense a quoted passage, you can use the ellipsis mark (three periods, with spaces between) to indicate that you have left words out. What remains must be grammatically complete.

Demski (2012) noted that "personalized learning . . . acknowledges and accommodates the range of abilities, prior experiences, needs, and interests of each student" (p. 33).

The writer has omitted the phrase *a student-centered teaching and learning model that* from the source.

When you leave out one or more full sentences, use a period before the three ellipsis dots.

According to Demski (2012), "In any personalized learning model, the student — not the teacher — is the central figure. . . . Personalized learning may finally allow individualization and differentiation to actually happen in the classroom" (p. 34).

Ordinarily, do not use an ellipsis mark at the beginning or at the end of a quotation. Readers will understand that you have taken the quoted material from a longer passage. The only exception occurs when you feel it necessary, for clarity, to indicate that your quotation begins or ends in the middle of a sentence.

USING SOURCES RESPONSIBLY: Make sure that omissions and ellipsis marks do not distort the meaning of your source.

Using brackets   Brackets allow you to insert your own words into quoted material to clarify a confusing reference or to make the quoted words fit grammatically into the context of your writing.

Demski's (2012) research confirms that "implement[ing] a true personalized learning model on a national level" is difficult for a number of reasons (p. 36).

To indicate an error such as a misspelling in a quotation, insert [*sic*], italicized and with brackets around it, right after the error.

Setting off long quotations   When you quote 40 or more words, set off the quotation by indenting it one-half inch from the left margin. Use the normal right margin and double-space the quotation.

Long quotations should be introduced by an informative sentence, often followed by a colon. Quotation marks are unnecessary because the indented format tells readers that the passage is taken from the source.

According to Svokos (2015), College and Education Fellow for *The Huffington Post,* some educational technology resources entertain students while supporting student-centered learning:

> GlassLab, a nonprofit that was launched with grants from the Bill & Melinda Gates and MacArthur Foundations, creates educational games that are now being used in more than 6,000 classrooms across the country. Some of the company's games are education versions of existing ones — for example, its first release was SimCity EDU — while others are originals. Teachers get real-time updates on students' progress as well as suggestions on what topics students need to spend more time on.

For a source with page numbers (unlike the example, which is an online source), the parenthetical citation with a page number goes outside the final mark of punctuation. (When a quotation is run into your text, the opposite is true. See the sample citations on the previous page.)

9b Using signal phrases to integrate sources

Whenever you include a direct quotation, a paraphrase, or a summary in your paper, prepare readers for it with a *signal phrase*. A signal phrase usually names the author of the source, gives the publication date in parentheses, and often provides some context. It is acceptable in APA style to call authors by their last name only, even on first mention. If your paper refers to two authors with the same last name, use their initials as well.

See the chart on the next page for a list of verbs commonly used in signal phrases.

NOTE: Use the past tense or present perfect tense to introduce quotations, other source material, and your own results: *Davis (2015) noted . . . , Manning (2017) has claimed . . . , males over 50 performed better than males aged 50 and under. . . .* Use the present tense to discuss the applications or effects of your own results or knowledge that has clearly been established: *the data suggest . . . , researchers agree. . . .*

Marking boundaries   Avoid dropping quotations into your text without warning. Provide clear signal phrases, including at least the author's name and the date of publication. Signal phrases mark the boundaries between source material and your own words and ideas.

DROPPED QUOTATION

Many educators have been intrigued by the concept of blended learning but have been unsure how to define it. "Blended learning is a formal education program in which a student learns at least in part through online delivery of content and instruction with some element of student control over time, place, and pace" (Horn & Staker, 2011, p. 4).

QUOTATION WITH SIGNAL PHRASE

Many educators have been intrigued by the concept of blended learning but have been unsure how to define it. As Horn and Staker (2011) have argued, "Blended learning is a formal education program in which a student learns at least in part through online delivery of content and instruction with some element of student control over time, place, and pace" (p. 4).

Integrating statistics and other facts   When you are citing a statistic or another specific fact, a signal phrase is often not necessary. In most cases, readers will understand that the citation refers to the statistic or fact (not the whole paragraph).

Using signal phrases in APA papers

To avoid monotony, try to vary both the language and the placement of your signal phrases.

Model signal phrases

In the words of Mitra (2013), ". . ."

As Bell (2010) has noted, ". . ."

Donitsa-Schmidt and Zuzovsky (2014), educational researchers, pointed out that ". . ."

". . .," claimed Çubukçu (2012).

". . .," wrote Demski (2012), ". . ."

Horn and Staker (2011) have offered a compelling argument for this view: ". . ."

Moeller and Reitzes (2011) answered these objections with the following analysis: ". . ."

Verbs in signal phrases

Are you providing background, explaining a concept, supporting a claim, lending authority, or refuting a belief? Choose a verb that is appropriate for the way you are using the source.

admitted	contended	reasoned
agreed	declared	refuted
argued	denied	rejected
asserted	emphasized	reported
believed	insisted	responded
claimed	noted	suggested
compared	observed	thought
confirmed	pointed out	wrote

Of polled high school students, 43% said that they lacked confidence in their technological proficiency going into college and careers (Moeller & Reitzes, 2011).

Putting source material in context   Provide context for any source material that appears in your paper. A signal phrase can help you connect your own ideas with those of another writer by clarifying how the source will contribute to your paper. It's a good idea to embed source material, especially long quotations, between sentences of your own that interpret the source and link the source to your own ideas.

QUOTATION WITH EFFECTIVE CONTEXT

According to the International Society for Technology in Education (2016), "Student-centered learning moves students from passive receivers of information to active participants in their own discovery process." The results of student-centered learning have been positive, not only for academic achievement but also for student self-esteem, because students actively participate in the process of learning.

9c Synthesizing sources

When you synthesize multiple sources in a research or an analytical paper (or any other paper that involves sources), you create a conversation about your topic. You show readers how the ideas of one source relate to those of another by connecting and analyzing the ideas in the context of your argument or discussion. Keep the emphasis on your own writing. The thread of your ideas should be easy to identify and to understand, with or without your sources.

In the following sample synthesis, student writer April Wang uses her own analysis to shape the conversation among her sources. She does not simply string quotations together or allow sources to overwhelm her writing. In the final sentence, she explains to readers how her sources support and extend her argument.

SAMPLE SYNTHESIS

1
2
It is clear that educational technology will continue to play a role in student and school performance. Horn and Staker (2011) acknowledged that they focused on programs in which integration of educational technology led to improved student performance. In other schools, technological learning is simply distance learning — watching a remote teacher — and not student-centered learning that allows students to partner with teachers to develop enriching learning experiences. That said, many educators seem convinced that educational technology has the potential to help them transition from traditional teacher-driven learning to student-centered learning.

Student writer

Source 1

Student writer

Continued ➜

3 All four schools in the Stanford study heavily relied on technology (Friedlaender et al., 2014). And indeed, Demski (2012) argued that technology is not supplemental but instead is "central" to student-centered learning (p. 33). | Source 2

| Source 3

4 Rather than turning to a teacher as the source of information, students are sent to investigate solutions to problems by searching online, emailing experts, collaborating with one another in a wiki space, or completing online practice. Rather than turning to a teacher for the answer to a question, students are driven to perform — driven to use technology to find those answers themselves. | Student writer

1 Student writer April Wang begins with a claim that needs support.

2 A signal phrase indicates how the source contributes to Wang's paper and shows that the ideas that follow are not her own.

3 Wang extends the argument and sets up two additional sources.

4 Wang closes the paragraph by interpreting the source and connecting it to her claim.

Formatting Papers in APA Style

10 Parts of a paper in APA style

This section describes the different parts of papers typically written in APA style. Not all of the parts described in this section are used in every genre, or type of paper. For example, method and results sections are typically included in laboratory reports but not in annotated bibliographies, professional memos, or reflective essays.

The chart on page 46 provides a quick overview of the parts that are typically used in each genre. If you have any doubt about which parts to include in a particular paper, check your assignment or ask your instructor.

10a Title page

Nearly all types of APA-style papers have a title page. It is always the first page and generally includes a running head, the title of the paper, the name of the author, and an author's note.

The title should briefly and accurately describe the purpose of the paper. The title should be concise yet specific and should not include unnecessary words such as "A Report on" or "A Paper About." Abbreviations should not be used in titles.

Effective titles indicate to the reader the main ideas, theories, or variables in a paper. For example, the title for the lab report on page 76—"Reaction Times for Detection of Objects in Two Visual Search Tasks"—includes information about the variables in the study (visual reaction times) as well as the methodology (visual search tasks). The title of the annotated bibliography on page 74—"Keynesian Policy: Implications for the Current U.S. Economic Crisis"—alerts the reader to the bibliography's theoretical perspective (Keynesian economic theory) and its subject (the current economic crisis).

For papers submitted for coursework, the author's note may include a few sentences that contain the title of the course, the name of the professor teaching the course, and any acknowledgments or thanks for assistance. Papers submitted for publication or for presentation at professional meetings may include additional information such as sources of grant money used to support the research and contact information for the author.

▶ Formatting the title page: **pp. 50–51**
▶ Sample title pages: **12a–12c, 12e–12k**

10b Abstract

An abstract is a short (150-to-250-word) summary of the content of the paper. Abstracts are generally used in literature reviews, empirical research papers, laboratory reports, and case studies. An abstract is always on the second page by itself. The purpose of the abstract is to provide an overview of the most important ideas of the paper, including the research question or hypothesis, methods, and key findings. In a paper prepared for publication, it is helpful to include key terms at the end of the abstract so that readers can find the paper online or in a database using a keyword search.

Even though the abstract appears at the beginning of the paper, some writers find it effective to write the abstract after writing a draft of the full paper. One way to approach writing the abstract is to ask yourself, "If someone read only my abstract, would the reader have a good understanding of the purpose of my paper and my most important findings and ideas?"

▶ Formatting the abstract: **p. 54**
▶ Sample abstracts: **12a, 12b, 12e, 12i**

10c Introduction

Most genres using APA style have an introduction, which begins on a new page following the abstract (or following the title page, if the paper does not have an abstract). The introduction is the first few paragraphs of the paper and typically contains a thesis statement or research question. In most papers, the introduction answers the questions "What is my paper about?" and "Why is it important?"

The introduction can frame the research question or thesis statement in relation to the work of others, in which case it also answers the question "What have others written about my topic?" In an empirical research paper, the introduction briefly describes how you conducted your study. Finally, the introduction lays the foundation for the rest of the paper by giving readers a sense of what to expect and what conclusions you will draw. You should reserve a full discussion of the implications of your research for the discussion section (see 10f).

As with abstracts, some writers prefer to write the introduction after drafting the entire paper.

▶ Formatting the introduction: **p. 54**
▶ Sample introductions: **12a–k**

10d Method

The method section is used in empirical research papers, laboratory reports, case studies, and sometimes clinical practice papers. It describes the details of the research design—how you conducted your study. Each discipline has its own methods of investigation,

Required sections in different types of papers

Type of paper	Title page	Abstract	Introduction	Method	Results	Discussion (Conclusion)	References	Footnotes	Headings	Appendices	Visuals
Literature review	●	●	●			●	●	◗	●		◗
Empirical research	●	●	●	●	●	●	●	◗	●	◗	●
Analytical essay	●	◗	●			◗	●	◗	◗	◗	◗
Annotated bibliography	◗					●					
Laboratory report	●	●	●	●	●	●	●	◗	●	◗	●
Administrative report	◗	◗	●			◗	◗	◗	●	◗	◗
Clinical practice paper	●	◗	●	◗	◗	◗	◗	◗	◗	●	◗
Reflective essay	●		●			◗	◗	◗	◗		
Professional memo			●			◗	◗	◗	◗		◗
Case study	●	●	●	●	●	●	●	◗	●	◗	◗
Social issue paper	●		●			●	●	◗	◗		◗

● Required in most papers   ◗ Required in some papers

so the particular contents of the method section will vary.

Anyone interested in replicating your study will rely on the method section to conduct his or her own research, so it is important that you include all relevant details of the research design. A good method section fully answers the question "How did I design my research and conduct my investigation?"

Writers often use subsections, labeled with subheadings, to organize the method section. Subsections might include specific information about procedures, participants, or materials.

Some details should not be included in the method section. If you collected data using a survey, for example, you might discuss general characteristics of the survey in the method section and include the survey questions as an appendix (see 10j).

▶ Sample method sections: **12b, 12e**

10e Results

Empirical research papers, laboratory reports, and case studies must include a results section, which contains an analysis of the data. Clinical practice papers sometimes include a results section. The method used in the study and the nature of your research question will determine the type of analysis you present in the results section.

Studies that have generated numerical data frequently use statistical analysis to determine whether statistically significant relationships exist between independent and dependent variables. Social and behavioral scientists refer to this type of study as *quantitative*. By contrast, observational field studies in sociology, anthropology, and education are examples of *qualitative* research.

The results section answers the question "What significant relationships exist between the important variables in my study?" You should present the results as clearly and succinctly as possible; charts, tables, figures, or other visuals can be a helpful way to present important data concisely (see 10k). Interpretation of the findings should be saved for the discussion section (see 10f).

Like the method section, the results section may include subsections to describe the data, the procedures used to analyze the data, and important findings. In the results section, you must acknowledge all relevant findings, even those that do not support your hypothesis, your research question, or the results you expected to find (see 2e).

▶ Sample results sections: **12b, 12e**

10f Discussion

A discussion section is used in empirical research papers, laboratory reports, and case studies. It is also frequently used in literature reviews, analytical essays, clinical practice papers, memos, reflective essays, administrative reports, and social issue papers; in these genres, it may be called a "conclusion."

In a paper involving research or an experiment, the purpose of the discussion section is to interpret the results in light of your research question or hypothesis. The discussion section attempts to answer the question "What do the findings or the data in my study mean?" In answering this question, you should reflect critically on the study as a whole, making connections between your study and previous studies and noting any ways in which your study might be improved. You should also discuss any unanticipated findings and, where appropriate, offer explanations for them. The following are other questions commonly addressed in the discussion section: "Was my sample adequate?" "Were my measures precise and appropriate?" "Were there any problems in my research design? If so, how might someone design a better study?" "Can the results of my study be generalized to larger (or other) populations?" "Given the findings of my study and the relevant literature, do any important questions remain unanswered?"

In other genres, the discussion section or conclusion is used to highlight important points, to summarize key ideas, or to make connections. In a literature review, for example, the discussion section or conclusion provides an opportunity to critically assess the findings of other studies and to draw conclusions in relation to your research question.

▶ Sample discussion section: **12e**
▶ Sample conclusion: **12k**

10g References

The reference section provides full bibliographic information for each source used in the paper so that an interested reader can locate the source. The reference section begins on a new page following the end of the body of the paper. Any paper that uses outside sources must include a reference list.

▶ Formatting the reference list: **11b and section 14**
▶ Sample reference lists: **12a, 12c, 12e, 12k**

10h Footnotes

Footnotes are used for additional information that is too long or complicated to include in the main text (see 15a). Footnotes should be used sparingly; in-text citations are the primary method of citing source material (see section 13). Footnotes are also used in tables and figures (see 15b).

▶ Formatting footnotes: **p. 54**
▶ Sample footnotes in text: **12c**
▶ Sample footnotes in tables: **12g**

10i Headings

Headings are used in APA papers to provide structure and organization. Headings can be used in any genre. Like an outline, the heading structure of a paper gives readers a sense of how the ideas are organized. In empirical research papers, laboratory reports, and case studies, three first-level headings are almost always included in the body of the paper: "Method," "Results," and "Discussion." Each of these first-level headings may have second- or third-level subheadings.

▶ Formatting headings: **p. 54**
▶ Sample headings: **12a, 12b, 12e, 12g–i**

10j Appendices

In almost any genre using APA style, some information may be important but too distracting to include in the main text of the paper and too long for a footnote. Such material can be placed in an appendix at the end of the paper following the reference list.

For example, if you developed a long survey to collect the data used in your study, you could include a copy of the survey questions, without any responses, as an appendix.

10k Visuals

Visuals include tables, figures, graphs, charts, images, or any other nontext content found in a paper. While visuals are not required in any genre, they are often a good way to summarize data or other results. For example, it is common to create tables that display the results of statistical analyses such as correlation and multiple regression. Other visuals commonly used in some fields are diagrams that show the anticipated and actual relationships between independent and dependent variables. The chart on pages 52–53 shows various types of visuals and suggests how they might be used in a paper.

While visuals provide a snapshot of important information, you should include a written description or interpretation of the information contained in any visual.

> ▶ Formatting visuals: **pp. 55–56**
> ▶ Sample visuals: **12a, 12b, 12e–g, 12i, 12k**

11 APA paper format

The American Psychological Association makes a number of recommendations for formatting a paper and preparing a list of references. The guidelines in this section are consistent with advice given in the *Publication Manual of the American Psychological Association*, 6th ed. (Washington, DC: APA, 2010) and with typical requirements for undergraduate papers in the social sciences, business, education, and nursing.

11a Formatting the paper

Title page   Begin at the top left with the words "Running head," followed by a colon and the title of your paper (shortened to no more than 50 characters) in all capital letters. Put the page number 1 flush with the right margin.

About halfway down the page, on separate lines, center the full title of your paper, your name, and your school's name. At the bottom of the page, you may add the heading "Author Note," centered, followed by a brief paragraph that lists specific information about the course or department or provides acknowledgments or contact information. (See section 12 for sample title pages.)

Font If your instructor does not require a specific font, choose one that is standard and easy to read (such as 12-point Times New Roman).

Page numbers and running head Number all pages with arabic numerals (1, 2, 3, and so on) in the upper right corner about one-half inch from the top of the page. Flush with the left margin and on the same line as the page number, type a running head consisting of the title of the paper (shortened to no more than 50 characters) in all capital letters. On the title page only, include the words "Running head" followed by a colon before the title. (See section 12 for examples of running heads and page numbers.)

Margins, line spacing, and paragraph indents Use margins of one inch on all sides of the page. Left-align the text. Double-space throughout the paper. Indent the first line of each paragraph and footnote one-half inch.

Capitalization, italics, and quotation marks In titles of works in the text of the paper, capitalize all words of four letters or more (and all nouns, pronouns, verbs, adjectives, and adverbs of any length). Capitalize the first word following a colon in a title or a heading. In the body of your paper, capitalize the first word after a colon only if the word begins a complete sentence.

Italicize the titles of books, periodicals, and other long works, including websites. Use quotation marks for titles of periodical articles, short stories, and other short works.

NOTE: APA has different requirements for titles in the reference list. See page 116.

Choosing visuals to suit your purpose

Pie chart

Pie charts compare a part or parts to the whole. Segments of the pie represent percentages of the whole (and always total 100 percent).

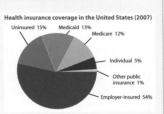

Health insurance coverage in the United States (2007)

Uninsured 15% Medicaid 13%
Medicare 12%
Individual 5%
Other public insurance 1%
Employer-insured 54%

Bar graph (or line graph)

Bar graphs highlight trends over a period of time or compare numerical data. Line graphs display the same data as bar graphs; the data are graphed as points, and the points are connected with lines.

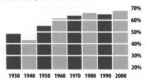

THE PURSUIT OF PROPERTY
Home ownership rates in the United States

70%
60%
50%
40%
30%
20%
1930 1940 1950 1960 1970 1980 1990 2000

Infographic

An infographic presents data in a visually engaging form. The data are usually numerical, as in bar graphs or line graphs, but they are represented by a graphic element instead of by bars or lines.

Just 8% of kids growing up in low-income communities graduate from college by age 24.

Table

Tables display numbers and words in columns and rows. They can be used to organize complicated numerical information into an easily understood format.

Prices of daily doses of AIDS drugs (\$US)

Drug	Brazil	Uganda	Côte d'Ivoire	US
3TC (Lamuvidine)	1.66	3.28	2.95	8.70
ddC (Zalcitabine)	0.24	4.17	3.75	8.80
Didanosine	2.04	5.26	3.48	7.25
Efavirenz	6.96	n/a	6.41	13.13
Indinavir	10.32	12.79	9.07	14.93
Nelfinavir	4.14	4.45	4.39	6.47
Nevirapine	5.04	n/a	n/a	8.48
Saquinavir	6.24	7.37	5.92	6.50
Stavudine	0.56	6.19	4.10	9.07
ZDV/3TC	1.44	7.34	n/a	18.78
Zidovudine	1.06	4.34	2.43	10.12

Source: UNAIDS, 2000

Diagram

Diagrams, useful in scientific and technical writing, concisely illustrate processes, structures, or interactions.

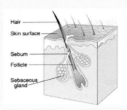

National Institutes of Health

Flowchart

Flowcharts show structures or steps in a process and their relation to one another.

Photograph

Photographs can be used to vividly depict people, scenes, or objects discussed in a text.

Library of Congress, Prints & Photographs Division, Reproduction Number LC-DIGhighsm-04024.

Map

Maps illustrate distances, historical information, or demographics and often use symbols for geographic features and points of interest.

Lynn Hunt et al., *The Making of the West.* Copyright © 2016 by Bedford/ St. Martin's. Reprinted by permission of Bedford/ St. Martin's.

Long quotations When a quotation is 40 or more words, set it off from the text by indenting it one-half inch from the left margin. Double-space the quotation. Do not use quotation marks around it. (See 12c or 12k for an example. See also p. 38 for more information about integrating long quotations.)

Footnotes If you insert a footnote number in the text of your paper, place the number immediately following any mark of punctuation except a dash. At the bottom of the page, begin the footnote with a one-half-inch indent and the superscript number corresponding to the number in the text. Insert an extra double-spaced line between the last line of text on the page and the footnote. Double-space the footnote. (See 12k for an example. See also section 15a for more details about footnotes.)

Abstract If your paper requires one, include an abstract after the title page. Center the word "Abstract" (in regular font, not boldface) one inch from the top of the page. Double-space the abstract and do not indent the first line.

For a paper prepared for publication, a list of keywords follows the abstract. On the line below the abstract, type the word "Keywords," indented and italicized, followed by a colon. Then list important words related to your paper. Check with your instructor for requirements in your course. (See section 12 for sample abstract pages.)

Introduction On a new page following the abstract, center the complete title of the paper one inch below the top of the page. The introduction immediately follows the title, with no heading. Begin the first paragraph of the introduction with a one-half-inch indent. (See also 10c.)

Headings Major (first-level) headings are centered and boldface. In research papers and laboratory reports, typical major headings are "Method," "Results," and "Discussion." In other types of papers, the major headings should be informative and concise, conveying the structure of the paper. Second-level headings are flush left and boldface. Third-level headings are indented and boldface, followed by a period and the text on the same line.

In first- and second-level headings, capitalize the first and last words and all words of four or more letters (and nouns, pronouns, verbs, adjectives, and adverbs of any length). In third-level headings, capitalize only the first word, any proper nouns, and the first word after a colon.

First-Level Heading Centered

Second-Level Heading Flush Left

    Third-level heading indented. Text immediately follows.

NOTE: Always type the title of the paper, the headings "Abstract" and "References," and appendix titles in regular font, not boldface.

Visuals APA classifies visuals as tables and figures (figures include graphs, charts, drawings, and photographs).

Tables Label each table with an arabic numeral (Table 1, Table 2) and provide a clear title. The label and title should appear on separate lines above the table, flush left and double-spaced. Type the table number in regular font; italicize the table title.

Table 2
Effect of Nifedipine (Procardia) on Blood Pressure in Women

If you have used data from an outside source or have taken or adapted the table from a source, give the source information in a note below the table. Begin with the word "Note," italicized and followed by a period. If you use lettered footnotes to explain specific data in the table, those footnotes begin on a new line after the source information. Begin each footnote with the superscript letter corresponding to the letter in the table; do not indent the first line. (See also 15b. See 12a, 12b, 12f, and 12g for examples of tables in papers.)

Figures Place the figure number and a caption below the figure, flush left and double-spaced. Begin with the word "Figure" and an arabic numeral, both italicized, followed by a period. Place the caption, not italicized, on the same line. If you have taken or adapted the figure from an outside source, give the source information immediately following the caption. Use the term "From" or "Adapted from" before the source information. (See also 15b. See 12b, 12e, 12i, and 12k for examples of figures in papers.)

11b Preparing the list of references

Begin your list of references on a new page at the end of the paper. Center the title "References" one inch from the top of the page. Double-space throughout. (See section 12 for sample reference lists and see section 14 for guidelines on how to cite specific types of sources in the reference list.)

Indenting entries Type the first line of each entry flush left and indent any additional lines one-half inch.

Alphabetizing the list Alphabetize the reference list by the last names of the authors (or editors); when a work has no author or editor, alphabetize by the first word of the title other than *A*, *An*, or *The*.

If you list two or more works by the same author, arrange the entries by year, the earliest first. If you include two or more works by the same author in the same year, arrange them alphabetically by title. Add the letters "a," "b," and so on in the parentheses after the year. For journal articles, use only the year and the letter: (2015a). For articles in magazines and newspapers, use the full date and the letter in the reference list: (2015a, July 17); use only the year and the letter in in-text citations.

Authors' names Invert all authors' names and use initials instead of first names. Separate the names with commas. For two to seven authors, use an ampersand (&) before the last author's name (see item 2 in section 14a). For eight or more authors, give the first six authors, three ellipsis dots, and the last author (see item 3 in section 14a).

Titles of books and articles Italicize the titles and subtitles of books. Do not italicize or use quotation marks around the titles of articles. Capitalize only the first word of the title and subtitle (and all proper nouns). Capitalize names of periodicals as you would capitalize them normally (see section 37c).

Abbreviations for page numbers Abbreviations for "page" and "pages" ("p." and "pp.") are used before page numbers of newspaper articles and articles in edited books (see item 14a in section 14b and item 29b in section 14c) but not before page numbers of articles in magazines and scholarly journals (see items 12–13 in section 14b).

Breaking a URL or DOI When a URL or a DOI (digital object identifier) must be divided, break it after a double slash or before any other mark of punctuation. Do not insert a hyphen, and do not add a period at the end. If you will post your project online or submit it electronically and you want to include live URLs for readers to click on, do not insert any line breaks.

12 Sample pages from papers in APA style

This section contains pages from 11 student papers from a range of social science and related disciplines — education, psychology, sociology, economics, criminology, nursing, business, and composition. The pages show typical APA style for organization and formatting as well as proper APA style for in-text citations and the reference list. The samples may be helpful as you write different types of papers for your courses.

12a Research paper: Literature review (education)

April Bo Wang, a student in an education course, wrote a research paper reviewing the literature on student-centered learning. Her paper describes what researchers have written about the benefits of student-centered learning; she also draws conclusions based on her reading of the literature.

Research paper: Literature review   **Title page**

1 Running head: TECHNOLOGY AND STUDENT-CENTERED LEARNING   1   **2**

3

Technology and the Shift From Teacher-Delivered

to Student-Centered Learning:

A Review of the Literature

April Bo Wang

Glen County Community College

Author Note

4   This paper was prepared for Education 107, taught by

Professor Gomez.

---

1 Short title, no more than 50 characters, in all capital
letters on all pages; words "Running head" on title page only.
2 Arabic page number on all pages. **3** Full title and writer's
name and affiliation, centered. **4** Author's note (optional) for
extra information.

(Annotations indicate APA-style formatting and effective writing.)

TECHNOLOGY AND STUDENT-CENTERED LEARNING   2 **1**

Abstract **2**

In recent decades, instructors and administrators have viewed **3**
student-centered learning as a promising pedagogical practice that
offers both the hope of increasing academic performance and a
solution for teacher shortages. Differing from the traditional model
of instruction in which a teacher delivers content from the front
of a classroom, student-centered learning puts the students at the
center of teaching and learning. Students set their own learning
goals, select appropriate resources, and progress at their own pace.
Student-centered learning has produced both positive results and
increases in students' self-esteem. Given the recent proliferation
of technology in classrooms, school districts are poised for success
in making the shift to student-centered learning. The question for
district leaders, however, is how to effectively balance existing
teacher talent with educational technology.

Keywords: digital learning, student-centered learning, **4**
personalized learning, education technology, transmissive, blended

1 Short title, no more than 50 characters, flush left; page
number flush right. **2** Abstract appears on separate
page; heading centered and not boldface. **3** Abstract is a
150-to-250-word overview of paper. **4** Keywords (optional)
help readers search for a published paper on the web or in a
database.

Research paper: Literature review **First text page**

1

Technology and the Shift From Teacher-Delivered

to Student-Centered Learning:

A Review of the Literature

In the United States, most public school systems are struggling with teacher shortages, which are projected to worsen as the number of applicants to education schools decreases (Donitsa-Schmidt & Zuzovsky, 2014, p. 420). Citing federal data, *The New York Times* reported a 30% drop in "people entering teacher   preparation programs" between 2010

2 and 2014 (Rich, 2015). Especially in science and math fields, the teacher shortage is projected to escalate in the next 10 years (Hutchison, 2012). In recent decades, instructors and administrators have viewed the practice of student-centered learning as one promising solution. Unlike traditional teacher-delivered (also called "transmissive") instruction, student-centered learning allows students to help direct their own education by setting their own goals and selecting appropriate resources for achieving those goals. Though student-centered learning might once have been viewed as an experimental solution in understaffed schools, it is gaining credibility as an effective pedagogical practice. What is also gaining momentum is the idea that technology might play a significant role in fostering student-centered learning. This literature review will examine three key questions:

3
1. In what ways is student-centered learning effective?
2. Can educational technology help students drive their own learning?
3. How can public schools effectively combine teacher talent and educational technology?

4 In the face of mounting teacher shortages, public schools should embrace educational technology that promotes student-centered learning in order to help all students become engaged and successful learners.

---

1 Full title, centered and not boldface. **2** Source provides background information and context. **3** Questions provide organization and are repeated as main headings. **4** Paper's thesis.

Research paper: Literature review **Table**

Table 1 **1**

Comparison of Two Approaches to Teaching and Learning **2**

Teaching and learning period	Instructor-centered approach	Student-centered approach
Before class	• Instructor prepares lecture/instruction on new topic. • Students complete homework on previous topic.	• Students read and view new material, practice new concepts, and prepare questions ahead of class. • Instructor views student practice and questions and identifies learning opportunities.
During class	• Instructor delivers new material in a lecture or prepared discussion. • Students—unprepared—listen, watch, take notes, and try to follow along with the new material.	• Students lead discussions of the new material or practice applying the concepts or skills in an active environment. • Instructor answers student questions and provides immediate feedback.
After class	• Instructor grades homework and gives feedback about the previous lesson. • Students work independently to practice or apply the new concepts.	• Students apply concepts/skills to more complex tasks, some of their own choosing, individually and in groups. • Instructor posts additional resources to help students.

Note. Adapted from "The Flipped Class Demystified," n.d., retrieved from **3** New York University website: https://www.nyu.edu/faculty/teaching -and-learning-resources/instructional-technology-support/instructional -design-assessment/flipped-classes/the-flipped-class-demystified.html

1 Table compares and contrasts two key concepts. **2** Table number and title on separate lines; title italic. **3** Note gives sources of data used in table. Format of note differs from format of reference list.

Research paper: Literature review **Reference list**

1 References

Bell, S. (2010). Project-based learning for the 21st century: Skills
for the future. *The Clearing House, 83*(2), 39-43.

Çubukçu, Z. (2012). Teachers' evaluation of student-centered
learning environments. *Education, 133*(1), 49-66.

2 Demski, J. (2012, January). This time it's personal. *THE Journal
(Technological Horizons in Education), 39*(1), 32-36.

3 Donitsa-Schmidt, S., & Zuzovsky, R. (2014). Teacher supply and
demand: The school level perspective. *American Journal of
Educational Research, 2*(6), 420-429.

4 Friedlaender, D., Burns, D., Lewis-Charp, H., Cook-Harvey, C. M.,
& Darling-Hammond, L. (2014). Student-centered schools:
Closing the opportunity gap [Research brief]. Retrieved from
Stanford Center for Opportunity Policy in Education website:
https://edpolicy.stanford.edu/sites/default/files/scope-pub
-student-centered-research-brief.pdf

5 Horn, M. B., & Staker, H. (2011). The rise of K-12 blended
learning. Retrieved from Innosight Institute website: http://
www.christenseninstitute.org/wp-content/uploads/2013/04
/The-rise-of-K-12-blended-learning.pdf

Hutchison, L. F. (2012). Addressing the STEM teacher shortage in
American schools: Ways to recruit and retain effective STEM
teachers. *Action in Teacher Education, 34*(5/6), 541-550.

International Society for Technology in Education. (2016).
Student-centered learning. Retrieved from http://www.iste.org
/standards/essential-conditions/student-centered-learning

Mitra, S. (2013, February). *Build a school in the cloud* [Video file].
Retrieved from https://www.ted.com/talks/sugata_mitra
_build_a_school_in_the_cloud?language=en

1 List of references on new page; heading centered and not
boldface. **2** List alphabetized by authors' last names (or by
titles for works with no authors). **3** All authors' names inverted,
with initials for first and middle name(s). **4** Work with up to
seven authors: all authors listed, with ampersand (&) before
last author's name. **5** First line of each entry left-aligned,
subsequent lines indented ½". Double-spaced throughout.

12b Research paper: Empirical research (psychology)

In a research methods course, Jessica Conderman conducted an experiment on taste sensitivity. Her paper reviews the literature on the topic and then reports on and analyzes her own results. Because her study involved human participants, she received approval from her school's institutional review board (IRB; see 2f).

Research paper: Empirical research   **Title page**

[1] Running head: INFLUENCES ON TASTE SENSITIVITY   1 **[2]**

The Influence of Sex and Learning on Taste Sensitivity   **[3]**

Jessica S. Conderman

Carthage College

Author Note   **[4]**

Jessica S. Conderman, PSYC 471-01 Advanced Research Methods, Dr. Leslie Cameron, Department of Psychology, Carthage College.

Thank you to the Department of Psychology and Quality of Life Committee for funding support.

[1] Short title, no more than 50 characters, in all capital letters on all pages; words "Running head" and colon on title page only. **[2]** Arabic page number on all pages. **[3]** Full title and writer's name and affiliation, centered. **[4]** Author's note (optional) for extra information.

(Annotations indicate APA-style formatting and effective writing.)

Research paper: Empirical research　　　　**Abstract**

2　　　　　　　　　　Abstract

Perceptual learning enhances a person's ability to detect specific stimuli after the person experiences exposure to the stimuli.

3 Perceptual learning has been observed in taste aversion, but it has not been extensively investigated in taste sensitivity. The current study examined the effect of perceptual learning in taste thresholds of females and males. I studied taste sensitivity

4 longitudinally, testing every other day for 1 month, in 6 young adults (3 males, 3 females) between 19 and 21 years of age. Taste thresholds were determined using an electrogustometer at 4 tongue locations (front-left, front-right, back-left, back-right) corresponding to the chorda tympani and glossopharyngeal nerves. Results indicate that males and females demonstrated a perceptual learning effect—thresholds decreased with practice—and were consistent with previous research that females' thresholds were lower than males' for all tongue locations. In contrast to previous research in olfaction (Dalton, Doolittle, & Breslin, 2002), both males and females "learned." However, females overall performed better in the task, which is consistent with the previous literature on the chemical senses.

5　　　*Keywords:* perceptual learning, taste aversion, taste sensitivity, sex differences

1 Short title, no more than 50 characters, flush left; page number flush right. **2** Abstract appears on separate page; heading centered and not boldface. **3** Abstract is 150-to-250-word overview of paper. **4** Numerals used for all numbers in abstract, even those under 10. **5** Keywords (optional) help readers search for a paper online or in a database.

Research paper: Empirical research   First text page

INFLUENCES ON TASTE SENSITIVITY   3

The Influence of Sex and Learning on Taste Sensitivity   **1**

The development of taste involves changes in taste preferences and aversions that are influenced by personal experiences. These can vary among cultures, age groups, and sexes (Nakazato, Endo, Yoshimura, & Tomita, 2002; Tomita & Ikeda, 2002). Through various experiences with different taste stimuli, people develop taste acuity (Scahill & Mackintosh, 2004). Taste acuity allows people to distinguish between different flavors and determine their taste preferences and aversions (Tomita & Ikeda, 2002). Taste sensitivity allows people to detect the differences between various stimuli, such as electric or hot and cold, through the nerves in the tongue (Nakazato et al., 2002). **3** The detection and differentiation of taste stimuli determine how people perceive food and develop dietary habits.   **2**

The main purpose of this study was to determine if   **4** perceptual learning occurs in taste sensitivity by measuring taste thresholds in the tongue. An electrogustometer delivered electric stimuli to participants' tongues. (The threshold is the minimum amount of current required to discriminate between two short pulses of current.) Perceptual learning has been found in taste aversion research but, to my knowledge, has not been examined directly in taste sensitivity measured through electrogustometry. But Lobb, Elliffe, and Stillman (2000) did suspect learning when taste thresholds continued to decrease as testing progressed after the initial 10 sessions were omitted. Taste aversion studies have shown that participants demonstrated a learning effect as they gained exposure to electric stimuli (Bennett & Mackintosh, 1999; Blair & Hall, 2003; Dwyer, Hodder, & Honey, 2004).   **5**

[Introduction continues with the writer's hypothesis and a review of the literature on various aspects of the writer's research.]

1 Full title, repeated and centered, not boldface. **2** First part of introduction provides background on writer's topic. **3** Second and subsequent citations to work with three to five authors use "et al." after first author's name. **4** Writer explains her purpose and establishes importance of her research in context of previous research. **5** Two or more sources in one parenthetical citation listed alphabetically and separated by semicolons.

Research paper: Empirical research **Text page**

model and determined that the electrogustometer had high test-retest reliability, but Lobb et al. (2000) found that electrogustometry test-retest reliability was questionable.

❶ **Method**

❷ **Participants**

Participants were recruited through the college resident assistant program. Each participant provided written consent prior to testing.

❸ Taste sensitivity was studied in six young adults (three males, three females), ranging from 19 to 21 years of age, for one month with no more than one day separating sessions. There were a total of 15 testing sessions per participant. All participants were screened prior to testing and reported being nonsmokers with no current medication intake.

Materials

❹ The Rion TR-06 electrogustometer with a 5-mm diameter stainless steel anode administered an electric stimulus directly to the tongue. The levels of electric current are listed in Table 1.

❺ Table 1

❻ *Electrogustometry Currents for Testing Taste Sensitivity*

dB	−6	−4	−2	0	2	4	6	8	10	12	14	16	18	20	22	24	26
µA	4	5	6.4	8	10	13	16	20	25	32	44	50	64	80	100	136	170

Note. The electrogustometry currents are shown in dB on the dial of the Rion TR-06 electrogustometer. The corresponding µA levels are as given in Kuga, Ikeda, Suzuki, & Takeuchi (2002).

❼ **Procedure**

Participants were instructed not to eat or drink anything besides water at least one hour prior to testing. During each trial, two low-level electric pulses were presented in quick succession to the same location

❶ Method section begins with main heading, centered and boldface. **❷** Second-level headings flush left and boldface. **❸** All numbers under 10, including number of participants, spelled out. **❹** Numbers for precise increments expressed in numerals with abbreviated units of measure. **❺** Short table appears immediately following its mention in the text. **❻** Table number and title appear above table; title italic. **❼** Procedure section explains in detail how writer conducted the experiment.

Research paper: Empirical research   Text page

INFLUENCES ON TASTE SENSITIVITY   8

on the tongue. One stimulus was a standard stimulus that remained constant at 4 μA, a very low current. The other stimulus was a test stimulus, which varied in intensity. All testing began with pulses at 4 μA and 13 μA. Participants responded by reporting which of the stimuli seemed stronger, generally through finger taps. Participants' tongues were tested on the four locations corresponding to the chorda tympani and glossopharyngeal nerves (front-left, front-right, back-left, back-right). Tongue locations were tested in the same sequence for every session, starting at the back-left and ending at the front-right. Stimulus duration was set at 0.5 s (Lobb et al., 2000). Sessions were held at approximately the same time of day for each participant throughout the study.

     After participants reported five consecutive correct responses (identifying which stimulus seemed stronger), a "reversal" occurred— the test stimulus became higher or lower than the previous test stimulus. For all reversals after the first, the strength of the test stimulus increased after one inaccurate response and decreased after two accurate responses (Frank, Hettinger, Barry, Gent, & Doty, 2003; Miller, Mirza, & Doty, 2002). Electric stimulation continued until   **1**
seven reversals occurred per location (Miller et al., 2002).   **2**

Statistical Analysis

     Taste thresholds were calculated for each participant using the geometric mean of the last four reversals in each session (Ajdukovic, 1991). Two analyses of variance (ANOVA) for repeated measures were used. The first $2 \times 2 \times 15$ design was used to determine the effect   **3**
and interactions of tongue location (back-front), sex (male-female), and number of sessions. The second $2 \times 2 \times 15$ design was used to determine the effect and interaction of tongue location (back left-right), sex, and number of sessions.

---

1 For first reference to sources with three to five authors, all authors' names are given. **2** For subsequent references to sources with three to five authors, the first author's name is followed by "et al." **3** Writer uses familiar terminology in the field and standard notation ($2 \times 2 \times 15$) to describe experiment design.

Research paper: Empirical research   **Text page**

INFLUENCES ON TASTE SENSITIVITY   9

1

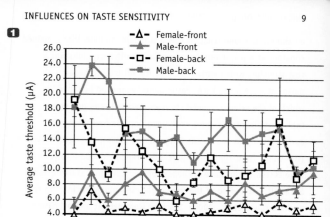

2 *Figure 1.* Perceptual learning in taste sensitivity in males and females, for front and back tongue locations. Error bars represent standard errors.

3   **Results**

The taste thresholds across trials for males and females in the back and front tongue locations are shown in Figure 1. Across sessions, taste thresholds (that is, the minimum current required to determine the difference between two pulses) decreased for males and females in the back tongue locations. A repeated-measures ANOVA revealed a main effect of session, **4** $F(1, 14) = 4.603$, $p = 0.000$, and location, $F(1, 1) = 22.843$, $p = 0.009$. There was also an interaction between session and **[Paper continues with the discussion section, which interprets the results of the experiment in the context of previous research, and ends with a reference list.]**

1 Figure presents data graphically for part of experiment. **2** Figure number and caption appear below figure. **3** Results section analyzes the data and uses figures to present the data graphically. **4** Writer uses standard notation to analyze data.

12c Analytical essay (sociology)

For a course in sociological theory, Hannah Elwell's assignment was to write an essay using several of Karl Marx's concepts and ideas to explain Walmart's economic success. Elwell's analysis draws on Marx's theories of exploitation of waged labor and fetishism of commodities.

Analytical essay	Title page

[1] Running head: SECRET OF WALMART'S SUCCESS: A MARXIAN ANALYSIS   1 **[2]**

The Secret of Walmart's Success: A Marxian Analysis   **[3]**

Hannah Elwell

University of Southern Maine

Author Note   **[4]**

This paper was prepared for SOC 300, Sociological Theory, taught by Professor Cheryl Laz.

---

[1] Short title, no more than 50 characters, in all capital letters on all pages; words "Running head" and colon on title page only. **[2]** Arabic page number on all pages. **[3]** Full title and writer's name and affiliation, centered. **[4]** Author's note (optional) for extra information.

(Annotations indicate APA-style formatting and effective writing.)

Analytical essay **First text page**

1 SECRET OF WALMART'S SUCCESS: A MARXIAN ANALYSIS 2

2 The Secret of Walmart's Success: A Marxian Analysis

3 What do big-screen TVs, bar soap, plastic building blocks, and strawberry toaster pastries have in common? All of these seemingly **4** disparate items—along with many more—can be found on the shelves of your local Walmart. The retail chain offers a stunning variety of consumer goods and groceries all under one roof, from electronics to apparel to cleaning supplies to frozen food. Walmart also offers certain services along with its products. A number of stores contain their own hair salons, photography studios, auto centers, or pharmacies, and some even provide health care, boasting walk-in clinics and vision centers where customers can receive eye examinations and other routine clinical services from independent health care professionals.

In every sense, Walmart is a massive corporation. The buildings that house the shelves full of consumer goods are colossal, with the average Walmart Supercenter measuring 185,000 **5** square feet ("About Us," n.d.). Walmart stores are large not just in size but also in number: There are more than nine thousand stores across 15 different countries, and they collectively employ 2.1 million people ("Walmart Stores," 2011). As the world's largest company, Walmart is enormously successful and powerful. Writer Charles Fishman (2007) noted in his article "The Wal-Mart You Don't Know"[1] that the retailer "does more business than Target, Sears, Kmart, J.C. Penney, Safeway, and Kroger combined."

So what is the secret to its economic success? Although Walmart is a modern phenomenon, the answer to this question can be found in the nineteenth-century teachings of one of modern economics' most influential thinkers, Karl Marx. From a Marxian perspective, Walmart can be seen as the epitome of capitalism. Its success is born from the

6 [1]In 2008, Wal-Mart changed the name of its stores to Walmart.

1 Short title, no more than 50 characters, flush left; page number flush right. **2** Full title, repeated and centered, not boldface. **3** Short analytical essay often does not require an abstract or headings. **4** Writer begins with engaging description. **5** Source with no author cited in text with first word or two of title; "n.d." for source with no date. **6** Footnote provides important explanation without interrupting text.

Analytical essay   **Text page**

SECRET OF WALMART'S SUCCESS: A MARXIAN ANALYSIS   3

exploitation of waged labor and the fetishism of commodities—two **1**
defining aspects of our modern capitalist, consumer culture.

The capitalist system is marked by a concentration of wealth
and resources—instead of being equally divided among all members
of society, wealth and resources end up in the hands of a select few
(the bourgeoisie), who then gain control over those with little or no
resources (the proletariat), thus creating class antagonism between
the two. In *The Communist Manifesto*, Marx (1848/2011) noted that **2**
industrial society was characterized by a "distinct feature: it has
simplified class antagonisms: Society as a whole is more and more
splitting up into two great hostile camps, into two great classes
directly facing each other: bourgeoisie and proletariat" (p. 53).

It is important to note that as a corporation and not a group
of people, Walmart does not have any actual class interests of its
own. However, those who stand to make a profit from Walmart's
capitalist enterprises are certainly members of the bourgeoisie and
thus are representatives of that class. Similarly, those who work for
Walmart are members of the proletariat. Thus, Walmart becomes a
perfect example of the class antagonism that Marx described in *The
Communist Manifesto*.

An examination of the ways in which these two classes work **3**
against each other is key to understanding how Walmart is so profitable.
In *Capital*, Marx (1867/2011) explained the difference between the ways
in which the owners (the bourgeoisie) and the workers (the proletariat)
relate to capital when he noted that "the circulation of commodities
is the starting-point of capital" (p. 73). However, for the bourgeoisie
and the proletariat, the form that this circulation takes is markedly
different. For the proletariat, it can be illustrated by the formula
C-M-C: exchanging a commodity (C) for money (M) and then
exchanging that money for another commodity (C). For the bourgeoisie,

1 Thesis sets up organization around two Marxian concepts.
2 For republished work, date of original publication is
given before date of publication of current source. **3** Topic
sentence provides transition to fuller explanation of "class
antagonism."

Analytical essay **Text page**

SECRET OF WALMART'S SUCCESS: A MARXIAN ANALYSIS 4

the formula changes to M-C-M', or exchanging money for a
commodity that is then exchanged for more money (M'). Marx
elaborated on this distinction:

1 > The circuit C-M-C starts with one commodity, and finishes
> with another, which falls out of circulation and into
> consumption. Consumption, the satisfaction of wants, in one
> word, use-value, is its end and aim. The circuit M-C-M, on
> the contrary, commences with money and ends with money.
> Its leading motive, and the goal that attracts it, is therefore
2 > mere exchange-value. (p. 74)

Of course, the bourgeoisie is not simply exchanging one sum of
money for the same sum of money, but rather for a greater sum.
In the case of the M-C-M' circuit, in Marx's words, "More money is
withdrawn from circulation at the finish than was thrown into it at
3 the start. . . . The . . . process is therefore M-C-M' . . . the original
sum advanced, plus an increment. This increment or excess over
the original value I call 'surplus-value'" (p. 74).

 This surplus-value is how Walmart makes its profit—spending
money to get commodities and then selling the commodities for a higher
price. The secret to this formula is production. Producers, or suppliers,
do not simply buy a commodity and then somehow sell that same
commodity back at a higher price. Rather, they buy commodities—for
example, cloth, thread, and cotton stuffing—and with them produce
a new commodity—perhaps a throw pillow—that they can then sell
for a new, higher price. As a retailer, Walmart does not produce its own
commodities, so it does in fact buy and then sell the same commodities
(the throw pillows, for example) at a profit. It counts on its suppliers
for the actual production work. Walmart also counts on its suppliers
(or rather, pressures them very strongly) to keep the cost of their
production work low so that Walmart can make a profit from the

1 Quotation of 40 or more words indented without quotation
marks. **2** Page number in parentheses after the final period.
3 Ellipsis mark indicates words omitted from source.

Analytical essay   **Reference list**

SECRET OF WALMART'S SUCCESS: A MARXIAN ANALYSIS   8

References **1**

About us. (n.d.). *Walmart corporate*. Retrieved from http:// **2**
  walmartstores.com/AboutUs/7606.aspx

Fishman, C. (2007, December 19). The Wal-Mart you don't know. **3**
  Fast Company. Retrieved from http://www.fastcompany.com
  /magazine/77/walmart.html

Marx, K. (2011). *Capital*. In S. Appelrouth & L. D. Edles, *Classical* **4**
  and contemporary sociological theory (pp. 63-76). Los
  Angeles, CA: Pine Forge Press. (Original work published 1867)

Marx, K. (2011). *The Communist manifesto*. In S. Appelrouth & **5**
  L. D. Edles, *Classical and contemporary sociological theory*
  (pp. 50-63). Los Angeles, CA: Pine Forge Press. (Original work
  published 1848)

Marx, K. (2011). *Economic and philosophic manuscripts of 1844*. **6**
  In S. Appelrouth & L. D. Edles, *Classical and contemporary*
  sociological theory (pp. 41-50). Los Angeles, CA: Pine Forge
  Press. (Original work published 1844)

Walmart Stores, Inc. data sheet: Worldwide unit details.
  (2011, April). *Walmart corporate*. Retrieved from http://
  walmartstores.com/pressroom/news/10594.aspx

1 List of references on new page; heading centered and not boldface. **2** Abbreviation "n.d." used for source with no date of publication or update. **3** List alphabetized by authors' last names or titles (for works with no authors). First line of each entry flush left; subsequent lines indented ½". Double-spaced throughout. **4** Authors' names inverted, with initial(s) for first name(s). **5** For older work contained in recent work, date of original publication given in parentheses at end of entry. **6** Two or more works by one author in same year alphabetized by title, with "a," "b," and so on after the year.

12d Annotated bibliography (economics)

Katie Niemeyer, a student in an intermediate macroeconomics course, prepared a reference list for a paper on the implications of Keynesian policy for the U.S. economy. She annotated each reference list entry by summarizing the source and then evaluating how it would apply to the topic of her paper.

Annotated bibliography   **First page**

---

1 Running head: KEYNESIAN POLICY: IMPLICATIONS FOR U.S. CRISIS   1 **2**

3 Katie Niemeyer

Professor Brent McClintock

2520 Intermediate Macroeconomics

4   Keynesian Policy: Implications for the Current U.S. Economic Crisis

5 Auerbach, A. J., Gale, W. G., & Harris, B. H. (2010). Activist fiscal

policy. *Journal of Economic Perspectives, 24*(4), 141-164.

6   This article provides a historical review of U.S. fiscal

policy in the last 30 years, including the activist policy

decisions made by the Obama administration in the economic

crisis starting in 2008. The authors chart the government's

economic tactics through time—from previous government

policies of fiscal restraint to the current activist policy that

supports the private sector. The article provides specific

information about President Obama's American Recovery and

Restoration Act and the Making Work Pay Credit. It addresses

the concerns and support for such policy decisions by fiscally

conservative classical economists as well as proponents of

Keynesian activist policies.

Bergsten, C. F. (2005). *The United States and the world economy.*

Washington, DC: Institute for International Economics.

---

1 Short title, no more than 50 characters, in all capital letters on all pages; words "Running head" and colon on first page only. **2** Arabic page number on all pages. **3** Writer's name, instructor, and course title, flush left. **4** Full title, centered and not boldface. **5** Each entry begins at left margin; subsequent lines indented ½". **6** Entire annotation indented ½"; first line indented additional ½".

(Annotations indicate APA-style formatting and effective writing.)

Annotated bibliography   **Text page**

KEYNESIAN POLICY: IMPLICATIONS FOR U.S. CRISIS   2 **1**

> Bergsten's book offers figures and graphs that will **2**
support my points about the productivity boom of the
1990s and the expansion of U.S. participation in the world
economy. Figure 2 demonstrates the positive role the
microprocessor played in U.S. economic expansion in the
1990s by showing the contribution of information technology
to GDP. Figure 3 demonstrates the incredible increase in U.S.
trade since 1960 owing to productivity growth and economic
deregulation of the global market. It graphically shows that
the U.S. trade/GDP ratio tripled from the 1960s to 2003.

Courtois, R. (2009, April). *What we do and don't know about
discretionary fiscal policy* (Report No. EB09-04). Retrieved
from the Federal Reserve Bank of Richmond website: http://
www.richmondfed.org/publications/research/economic
_brief/2009/pdf/eb_09-04.pdf

> This economic brief published by the Federal Reserve **3**
Bank of Richmond outlines the United States' expansive use
of discretionary fiscal policy in the current economic crisis,
while at the same time explaining why classical economists
disagree with such measures. Supporting the nondiscretionary
tendencies of classical theorists, Courtois (2009) wrote, **4**
"The current recession was not identified as such by the
National Bureau of Economic Research until December 2008,
a full year after it began" (p. 3). The discussion of specific
concerns with the Obama administration's stimulus packages
and discretionary fiscal policy, in both the long and the short
run, can help me present multiple viewpoints in my paper.

[Writer continues with five more annotated sources.]

1 Short title, no more than 50 characters, flush left; page
number flush right on all pages. **2** Writer assesses how
source will be useful in her paper. **3** Double-spaced
throughout. **4** Quotation captures major point of report;
writer includes page number for direct quotation.

12e Laboratory report (psychology)

Allison Leigh Johnson conducted a cognition experiment for a laboratory assignment in a psychology course. Her experiment focused on participants' reaction times in detecting objects in a variety of situations. Because this experiment was conducted in a classroom setting, Johnson did not have to seek approval from an institutional review board (IRB; see 2f).

Laboratory report   **Title page**

1 Running head: REACTION TIMES IN TWO VISUAL SEARCH TASKS   1 **2**

3 Reaction Times for Detection of Objects in Two Visual Search Tasks

Allison Leigh Johnson

Carthage College

4   Author Note

Allison Leigh Johnson, Department of Psychology, Carthage
College. This research was conducted for Psychology 2300,
Cognition: Theories and Application, taught by Professor Leslie
Cameron.

---

1 Short title, no more than 50 characters, in all capital
letters on all pages; words "Running head" and colon on title
page only. **2** Arabic page number on all pages. **3** Full title
and writer's name and affiliation, centered. **4** Author's note
(optional) for extra information.

(Annotations indicate APA-style formatting and effective writing.)

Laboratory report   **Abstract**

REACTION TIMES IN TWO VISUAL SEARCH TASKS   2 **1**

Abstract **2**

Visual detection of an object can be automatic or can require
attention. The reaction time varies depending on the type of
search task being performed. In this visual search experiment,
3 independent variables were tested: type of search, number of **3**
distracters, and presence or absence of a target. A feature search
contains distracters notably different from the target, while a
conjunctive search contains distracters with features similar to **4**
the target. For this experiment, 14 Carthage College students
participated in a setting of their choice. A green circle was the
target. During the feature search, reaction times were similar
regardless of the number of distracters and the presence or absence
of the target. In the conjunctive search, the number of distracters
and the presence or absence of the target affected reaction times.
This visual search experiment supports the idea that feature
searches are automatic and conjunctive searches require attention
from the viewer.

    Keywords: visual search, cognition, feature search, **5**
conjunctive search

1 Short title, no more than 50 characters, flush left; page
number, flush right. **2** Abstract appears on separate page;
heading centered and not boldface. **3** Numerals used for
all numbers in abstract, even those under 10. **4** Abstract is
150-to-250-word overview of paper. **5** Keywords (optional)
help readers search for a paper online or in a database.

Laboratory report   **First text page**

REACTION TIMES IN TWO VISUAL SEARCH TASKS   3

❶ Reaction Times for Detection of Objects in Two Visual Search Tasks

❷   Vision is one of the five senses, and it is the sense trusted most by humans (Reisberg, 2010). We use our vision for everything. We are always looking for things, whether it is where we are going or finding a friend at a party. Our vision detects the object(s) we are looking for. Some objects are easier to detect

❸ than others. Spotting your sister wearing a purple shirt in a crowd of boring white shirts is automatic and can be done with ease. However, if your sister was also wearing a white shirt, it would take much time and attention to spot her in that same crowd.

     The "pop out effect" describes the quick identification of an object being searched for because of its salient features (Reeves, 2007). When you look for your sister wearing a purple shirt, for example, you use the pop out effect for quick identification. The pop out effect works when attention is drawn to a specific object that is different from the surrounding objects.

     Two types of searches are used to scan an environment, the feature search and the conjunctive search (Reeves, 2007). The feature search is simply scanning the environment for the feature or features of a target. The conjunctive search is scanning for a combination of features (Reeves, 2007). Other objects that possess one of the features being searched for are called *distracters*. Distracters, as the name suggests, draw one's attention away from the target. When one object is being searched for in a sea of repetitious different objects, the target is easily found because it is unique. As more distracters are added, the time to detect the target increases (Wolfe, 1998).

     Treisman's (1986) feature integration theory explained that single-feature searches are easy because they are automatic and that attention is required when more features are added because these items must be mentally constructed. This is demonstrated in visual

❶ Full title, repeated and centered, not boldface.
❷ Introduction briefly describes previous research on topic and provides background on writer's experiment. ❸ Writer uses second-person pronouns (*you*, *your*) in an everyday example to explain a complex concept.

Laboratory report   **Text page**

REACTION TIMES IN TWO VISUAL SEARCH TASKS   4

search experiments. The purpose of a visual search experiment is for
the participant to identify the target as fast as possible. In my visual
search experiment, the target was a green circle. The hypothesis of **1**
the experiment was that the green circle would be easier to detect
in a feature search than in a conjunctive search because, according
to Treisman's theory, attention is needed for the latter task.

Method   **2**
                                                               3
Participants

Fourteen Carthage College undergraduates participated. Four
were male. All were 19 to 21 years old.

Materials   **4**

The experiment was conducted in an environment of each
participant's choice, typically in a classroom or library, using the
ZAPS online psychology laboratory (2004).

Procedure

In the feature search, orange squares were the distracters,
and a green circle was the target. The conjunctive search contained
distracters of orange circles, green squares, and orange squares,
with the green circle as the target. For every trial under both
searches, either four, 16, or 64 stimuli were present on the screen. **5**
If the green circle was present, the participant pressed the _M_ key,
and if it was not present the _C_ key. There were 24 trials for each
search, and feedback was given by the online program after each.

Variables

The three independent variables were number of distracters
present, type of search, and presence or absence of the target. The
dependent variable was the reaction time.

Results   **6**

The reaction times in the feature search were constant regardless

---

1 Hypothesis at end of introduction. **2** Method heading
(first-level heading) centered and boldface. **3** Method section
presents details about how writer conducted her experiment.
4 Second-level headings flush left and boldface. **5** Numerals
(except when used to begin a sentence) for all numbers 10
and above; numbers below 10 spelled out. **6** Results section
describes data writer collected.

Laboratory report   **Text page**

REACTION TIMES IN TWO VISUAL SEARCH TASKS   5

of the presence of the target and the number of distracters. The
reaction times varied in the conjunctive search depending on the
presence of the target and the number of distracters. Reaction
times increased as the number of distracters increased, and reaction
[1] times were longer when the target was not present. Figure 1 shows
the reaction times based on the three independent variables.

[2]   **Discussion**

The way the three variables interacted greatly affected
the times needed by participants to find the target. The data in
Figure 1 show similar reaction times for the feature search and
varying reaction times for the conjunctive search. In the feature
search, the reaction times, regardless of the two variables, were
constant. In the conjunctive search, the reaction times were higher
when there were more distracters and even higher when the target
was not present. Without the target, participants scanned most of
the screen to try to detect the green circle, which is more time-
consuming than when the target is present. Reaction times also
increased as the number of distracters increased.

[3]   The results were primarily as expected. In Wolfe's (1998) study
of visual search, the slope of the feature search graph was significantly
lower than the slopes of the conjunctive search graphs. The slower
reaction time shown in Figure 1 for the conjunctive search is consistent
[4] with Wolfe's findings. The results of this visual search experiment
provide more evidence of the difference between the two types of
searches found in previous studies. The results support Treisman's
(1986) feature integration theory. Detecting a target among distracters
in the feature search is automatic—attention is not necessary. Treisman
also stated that to detect a target among two or more distracters,
attention is needed to piece together all of the features. This "mental

[1] Writer explains results in text and presents numerical
results graphically in figure. **[2]** Discussion section analyzes
and interprets results of experiment. **[3]** Writer analyzes data
in context of her hypothesis and other researchers' results.
[4] When author is cited two (or more) times in text of one
paragraph, date is not included in parentheses in subsequent
citations.

REACTION TIMES IN TWO VISUAL SEARCH TASKS　　　　　　6

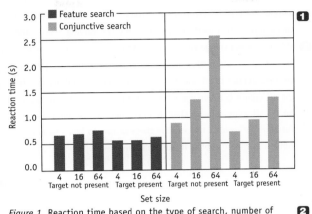

Figure 1. Reaction time based on the type of search, number of distracters (set size), and presence or absence of the target. Total experiments: 14; collected trials: 702.

gluing" of features requires attention, which in turn takes time. This is also shown in Figure 1. The reaction times, as predicted by Treisman's theory, increased when the number of distracters increased. Visual search explains why searching for clothes, people, cars, and so on takes various amounts of time depending on the target. It takes less time, because of automaticity, to detect a target with a single, standout feature than it would to detect a target with a number of features.

My study, however, does not account for the position of the target and the distracters on the screen. The position of the target could alter the reaction times if, for example, the target was always near the top where a person would most likely start scanning the environment. More visual search experiments could include

❶ Figure presents experiment data in bar graph. **❷** Figure title and caption below figure. **❸** Figure caption includes brief description of source of data. **❹** Writer discusses limitations of her experiment and suggests other variables that might be investigated.

Laboratory report   **Text page**

REACTION TIMES IN TWO VISUAL SEARCH TASKS   7

more distracters or even change distracters to see how the reaction times differ. This experiment covered only two varying objects and

1 shapes, a fairly simple environment. More complex visual search experiments could further investigate the theory Treisman (1986) believed applies to all searches. My experiment did not account for the difference between eye movement and head movement to search for the stimulus, a factor that could change the reaction times. Future experiments could explore these factors to test whether Treisman's theory applies in all situations.

1 Writer suggests directions for future research.

Laboratory report   **Reference list**

REACTION TIMES IN TWO VISUAL SEARCH TASKS   8

                          References   **1**

Reeves, R. (2007). *The Norton psychology labs workbook*. New York, **2**
        NY: Norton.

Reisberg, D. (2010). *Cognition: Exploring the science of the mind*.
        New York, NY: Norton.

Treisman, A. (1986). Features and objects in visual processing. **3**
        Scientific American, 255, 114-125.

Wolfe, J. M. (1998). What do 1,000,000 trials tell us about visual **4**
        search? *Psychological Science, 9*, 33-39.

ZAPS: The Norton psychology labs. (2004). Retrieved from **5**
        http://wwnorton.com/ZAPS/

1 List of references on new page; heading centered and not
boldface. **2** List alphabetized by authors' last names, corporate
names, or titles (for works with no authors). **3** Authors' names
inverted, with initial(s) for first name(s). **4** First line of each entry
flush left; subsequent lines indented ½". **5** Double-spaced
throughout.

12f Administrative report (criminology/ criminal justice)

For a course on crime and crime policy, Chris Thompson was asked to write a report on crime in his hometown, as if he were briefing a new chief of police. Thompson's report presents and analyzes local crime statistics and compares the town's data to federal crime statistics.

Administrative report   **Title page**

1 Running head: CRIME IN LEESBURG, VIRGINIA   1 **2**

3

Crime in Leesburg, Virginia

Chris Thompson

George Mason University

4   Author Note

This paper was prepared for Administration of Justice 305:

Crime Policy, taught by Professor Devon Johnson.

---

1 Short title, no more than 50 characters, in all capital letters on all pages; words "Running head" and colon on title page only. **2** Arabic page number on all pages. **3** Full title and writer's name and affiliation, centered. **4** Author's note (optional) for extra information.

(Annotations indicate APA-style formatting and effective writing.)

CRIME IN LEESBURG, VIRGINIA   2   **1**

Crime in Leesburg, Virginia   **2**

3   This report reviews crime statistics in Leesburg, Virginia, to familiarize the new police chief with the town and offer some suggestions about where to focus law enforcement resources. It analyzes local and national statistics from the FBI's Uniform Crime Reports (UCR) for the United States and for Leesburg and offers a basic assessment of the town's needs to provide a useful snapshot for the chief of police.

Description of Leesburg, Virginia   **4**

    Leesburg, Virginia, is a suburb of Washington, DC, 40 miles to the northwest. In 2008, its population was 39,899 (U.S. Department of Justice, 2009, Table 8). Like many northern Virginia and southern Maryland communities, it serves as a suburban bedroom community to those employed in the nation's capital. The town has grown significantly in the last three decades.

5   Leesburg's population is predominantly middle and upper middle class, with a median household income 75% higher than the national average (Town of Leesburg, Virginia, 2009a). Leesburg is populated by young (median age 32.3), well-educated (about 50% with a bachelor's degree, about 17% with an advanced degree) citizens; half are white-collar professionals (Town of Leesburg, Virginia, 2009a).

    The Leesburg Police Department has 77 sworn officers, operates 24 hours a day, and uses numerous special teams and modern law enforcement techniques. The department has divided the city into three patrol areas to address the specific needs of each zone (Town of Leesburg, Virginia, 2009b).

Nature and Extent of Crime in Leesburg, Virginia

    Tables 1 and 2 show the FBI's UCR statistics for 2008. Table 1   **6** contains statistics for Leesburg and the United States, and Table 2

---

1 Short title, no more than 50 characters, flush left; page number flush right. **2** Full title, repeated and centered, not boldface. **3** Introduction gives purpose of report and acknowledges audience. **4** Main headings (first-level headings), centered and boldface, define major sections of report. **5** Demographic information provides background for statistics in next section. **6** Writer refers in text to data tables.

Administrative report   **Text page**

CRIME IN LEESBURG, VIRGINIA   3

1 Table 1

Crime Rates, by Crime, in Leesburg, Virginia, and in the United States, 2008

Offense type	Leesburg		United States	
	No. reported offenses	Rate per 100,000 inhabitants	No. reported offenses	Rate per 100,0000 inhabitants
Violent crime				
Forcible rape	7	17.5	89,000	29.3
Murder and nonnegligent manslaughter	1	2.5	16,272	5.4
Robbery	22	55.1	441,855	145.3
Aggravated assault	29	72.7	834,885	274.6
Total violent crime	59	147.8	1,382,012	454.5
Property crime				
Larceny theft	715	1,792	6,588,873	2,167
Burglary	62	155.4	2,222,196	730.8
Vehicle theft	25	62.7	956,846	314.7
Total property crime	802	2,010	9,767,915	3,212.5

Note. The data for Leesburg, Virginia, are from U.S. Department of Justice (2009), Table 8. The data for the United States are from U.S. Department of Justice (2009), Table 1.

presents the crime rate in Leesburg as a percentage of the national average. A discussion of the accuracy of the UCR is on page 5.

3 **Crime Rates in Leesburg Compared With the National Average**

The following list of index crimes compares their rates in Leesburg, Virginia (first value), with the national average (second value). In general, the crime rate in Leesburg is lower than it is across the country. This may be due in part to the demographics of the town's residents and the commuter-oriented suburban nature of the community.

1 Table number and title above table; table title italic.
2 Clearly labeled data categories reinforce writer's purpose.
3 Main section of report analyzes details from tables. Section is divided into subsections, with second-level headings (not shown), that discuss the specific crime statistics listed in Table 1.

12g Clinical practice paper (nursing)

Julie Riss, a student in a nursing class focused on clinical experience, wrote a practice paper in which she provides a detailed client history, her assessment of the client's condition, nursing diagnoses of the client's health issues, her own recommendations for interventions, and her rationales for the interventions.

Clinical practice paper	Title page

[1] Running head: ALL AND HTN IN ONE CLIENT   1 [2]

Acute Lymphoblastic Leukemia and Hypertension in One Client: [3]

A Nursing Practice Paper

Julie Riss

George Mason University

Author Note   [4]

This paper was prepared for Nursing 451, taught by Professor Durham. The author wishes to thank the nursing staff of Milltown General Hospital for help in understanding client care and diagnosis.

[1] Short title, no more than 50 characters, in all capital letters on all pages; words "Running head" and colon on title page only. [2] Arabic page number on all pages. [3] Full title and writer's name and affiliation, centered. [4] Author's note (optional) for extra information.

(Annotations indicate APA-style formatting and effective writing.)

Clinical practice paper **First text page**

1 ALL AND HTN IN ONE CLIENT 2

2 Acute Lymphoblastic Leukemia and Hypertension in One Client:

A Nursing Practice Paper

3 **Historical and Physical Assessment**

4 **Physical History**

E.B. is a 16-year-old white male 5'10" tall weighing 190 lb. He
was admitted to the hospital on April 14, 2006, due to decreased
platelets and a need for a PRBC transfusion. He was diagnosed in
October 2005 with T-cell acute lymphoblastic leukemia (ALL), after
5 a 2-week period of decreased energy, decreased oral intake, easy
bruising, and petechia. The client had experienced a 20-lb weight loss
in the previous 6 months. At the time of diagnosis, his CBC showed a
WBC count of 32, an H & H of 13/38, and a platelet count of 34,000.
He began induction chemotherapy on October 12, 2005, receiving
vincristine, 6-mercaptopurine, doxorubicin, intrathecal methotrexate,
and then high-dose methotrexate per protocol. During his hospital stay
he required packed red cells and platelets on two different occasions. He
was diagnosed with hypertension (HTN) due to systolic blood pressure
readings consistently ranging between 130s and 150s and was started
on nifedipine. E.B. has a history of mild ADHD, migraines, and deep
vein thrombosis (DVT). He has tolerated the induction and consolidation
phases of chemotherapy well and is now in the maintenance phase.

6 **Psychosocial History**

There is a possibility of a depressive episode a year
previously when he would not attend school. He got into serious
trouble and was sent to a shelter for 1 month. He currently lives
with his mother, father, and 14-year-old sister.

Family History

Paternal: prostate cancer and hypertension in grandfather
Maternal: breast cancer and heart disease

1 Short title, no more than 50 characters, flush left; page
number flush right. **2** Full title, repeated and centered,
not boldface. **3** First-level heading, boldface and centered.
4 Second-level heading, boldface and flush left. **5** Writer's
summary of client's medical history. **6** Headings guide
readers and define sections.

Clinical practice paper   **Text page**

ALL AND HTN IN ONE CLIENT   3

Current Assessment   ❶

     Client's physical exam reveals him to be alert and oriented to
person, place, and time. He communicates, though not readily. His
speech and vision are intact. He has an equal grip bilaterally and can
move all extremities, though he is generally weak. Capillary refill is less   ❷
than 2 s. His peripheral pulses are strong and equal, and he is positive
for posterior tibial and dorsalis pedis bilaterally. His lungs are clear to
auscultation, his respiratory rate is 16, and his oxygen saturation is
99% on room air. He has positive bowel sounds in all quadrants, and
his abdomen is soft, round, and nontender. He is on a regular diet,
but his appetite has been poor. Client is voiding appropriately, and his
urine is clear and yellow. He appears pale and is unkempt. His skin is
warm, dry, and intact. He has alopecia as a result of chemotherapy. His
mediport site has no redness or inflammation. He appears somber and
is slow to comply with nursing instructions.

**[The writer includes two sections, not shown, describing the
client's diagnoses.]**

Rationale for Orders

     Vital signs are monitored every four hours per unit standard. In   ❸
addition, the client's hypertension is an indication for close monitoring
of blood pressure. He has generalized weakness, so fall precautions
should be implemented. Though he is weak, ambulation is important,
especially considering the client's history of DVT. A regular diet is
ordered—I'm not sure why the client is not on a low-sodium diet, given
his hypertension. Intake and output monitoring is standard on the
unit. His hematological status needs to be carefully monitored due to
his anemia and thrombocytopenia; therefore he has a CBC with manual
differential done each morning. In addition, his hematological status is
checked posttransfusion to see if the blood and platelets he receives

❶ Detailed assessment of client. ❷ Writer uses neutral
tone and appropriate medical terminology. ❸ Physiology,
prescribed treatments, and nursing practices are applied in
this section.

Clinical practice paper   **Text page**

ALL AND HTN IN ONE CLIENT   6

1   **Pharmacological Interventions and Goals**

2 *Medications and Effects*

3

ondansetron hydrochloride (Zofran) 8 mg PO PRN	serotonin receptor antagonist, antiemetic—prevention of nausea and vomiting associated with chemotherapy
famotidine (Pepcid) 10 mg PO ac	H2 receptor antagonist, antiulcer agent—prevention of heartburn
nifedipine (Procardia) 30 mg PO bid	calcium channel blocker, antihypertensive—prevention of hypertension
enoxaparin sodium (Lovenox) 60 mg SQ bid	low-molecular-weight heparin derivative, anticoagulant—prevention of DVT
mercaptopurine (Purinethol) 100 mg PO qhs	antimetabolite, antineoplastic—treatment of ALL
PRBCs—2 units leukoreduced, irradiated[a]	to increase RBC count

[a]Because these products are dispensed by pharmacy, they are considered pharmacological interventions, even though technically not medications.

4   **Laboratory Tests and Significance**

Complete Blood Count (CBC)[a]

Result name	Result	Abnormal	Normal range
WBC	3.0	*	4.5-13.0
RBC	3.73	*	4.20-5.40
Hgb	11.5		11.1-15.7
Hct	32.4	*	34.0-46.0
MCV	86.8		78.0-95.0
MCH	30.7		26.0-32.0
MCHC	35.4		32.0-36.0
RDW	14.6		11.5-15.5
Platelet	98	*	140-400
MPV	8.3		7.4-10.4

[a]*Rationale:* Client's ALL diagnosis and treatment necessitate frequent monitoring of his hematological status. WBC count, RBC, and hematocrit are decreased due to chemotherapy. The platelet count is low.

1 Main section heading, centered and boldface. **2** Short tables placed within text of paper; no table number necessary. **3** Two columns display client's medications and possible side effects. **4** Table presents client's lab reports.

12h Reflective essay (education)

For a service learning course exploring issues of diversity, power, and opportunity in school settings, Onnalee Gibson wrote about her experiences working with an 11th-grade student. She used professional sources to inform her ideas, but the essay is focused on her own reflections on the experience.

Reflective essay	Title page

[1] Running head: SERVICE LEARNING: ERIC   1 [2]

A Reflection on Service Learning: [3]
Working With Eric
Onnalee L. Gibson
Michigan State University

Author Note   [4]
This paper was prepared for Teacher Education 250, taught by Professor Carter. The author wishes to thank the guidance staff of Waverly High School for advice and assistance.

[1] Short title, no more than 50 characters, in all capital letters on all pages; words "Running head" and colon on title page only. [2] Arabic page number on all pages. [3] Full title and writer's name and affiliation, centered. [4] Author's note (optional) for extra information.

(Annotations indicate APA-style formatting and effective writing.)

Reflective essay **First text page**

1 SERVICE LEARNING: ERIC 2

2 A Reflection on Service Learning:

Working With Eric

3 The first time I saw the beautiful yet simple architecture of Waverly High School, I was enchanted. I remember driving by while exploring my new surroundings as a transfer student to Michigan State University and marveling at the long front wall of reflective windows, the shapely bushes, and the general cleanliness of the school grounds. When I was assigned to do a service learning project in a local school district, I hoped for the opportunity to find out what it would be like to work at a school like Waverly—a school where the attention to its students' needs was evident from the outside in.

4 Waverly High School, which currently enrolls about 1,100 students in Grades 9 through 12 and has a teaching staff of 63, is extremely diverse in several ways. Economically, students range from poverty level to affluent. Numerous ethnic and racial groups are represented. And in terms of achievement, the student body boasts an assortment of talents and abilities.

The school provides a curriculum that strives to meet the needs of each student and uses a unique grade reporting system that itemizes each aspect of a student's grade. The system allows both teachers and parents to see where academic achievement and academic problems surface. Unlike most schools, which evaluate students on subjects in one number or letter grade, Waverly has a report card that lists individual grades for tests, homework, exams, papers, projects, participation, community service, and attendance. Thus, if a student is doing every homework assignment and is still failing tests, this breakdown of the grades may effectively highlight how the student can be helped.

5 It was this unique way of evaluating students that led to my

1 Short title, no more than 50 characters, flush left; page number flush right. **2** Full title, repeated and centered, not boldface. **3** Writer begins with descriptive passages. **4** Background about school sets scene for personal experiences. **5** Transition from background to personal experiences.

12i Investigative report (business)

Brian Spencer, a student in an introductory business course, wrote an investigative report on the problem of employee motivation at a small company. His report combines research from outside sources, facts about the company's situation, and information from interviews with employees and management. It concludes with his recommendations.

Investigative report   **Title page**

1

2

Positively Affecting Employee Motivation   **3**

Prepared by Brian Spencer

Report Distributed March 9, 2006

Prepared for OAISYS   **4**

---

1 Formatting of all pages of report consistent with typical style in business. **2** Title page counted in numbering, but no page number appears. **3** Title, writer's name, and date centered. **4** Company name centered at bottom of page.

(Annotations indicate business-style formatting and effective writing.)

Investigative report **Abstract**

❷ **Abstract**

Corporate goals, such as sales quotas or increases in market share, do not always take into account employee motivation. Motivating employees is thus a challenge and an opportunity for firms that want to outperform their competitors. For a firm to achieve its goals, its employees must be motivated to perform effectively.

❸ Empirical research conducted with employees of a subject firm, OAISYS, echoed theories published by leading authorities in journals, books, and online reports. These theories argue that monetary incentives are not the primary drivers for employee motivation. Clear expectations, communication of progress toward goals, accountability, and public appreciation are common primary drivers. A firm aiming to achieve superior performance should focus on these activities.

❶ Page formatted in typical business style. Short title and page number flush right. ❷ Abstract on separate page; heading flush left and boldface. ❸ Paragraphs separated by extra line of space; first line of paragraph not indented.

Employee Motivation 3

Introduction   **1**

All firms strive to maximize performance. Such performance is
typically defined by one or more tangible measurements such as
total sales, earnings per share, return on assets, and so on. The
performance of a firm is created and delivered by its employees.
Employees, however, are not necessarily motivated to do their part
to maximize a firm's performance. Factors that motivate employees
can be much more complex than corporate goals. This report will
define the problem of employee motivation in one company and
examine potential solutions.

OAISYS is a small business based in Tempe, Arizona, that manufactures
business call recording products. Currently OAISYS employs 27
people. The business has been notably successful, generating annual
compound sales growth of over 20% during the last three years. The
company's management and board of directors expect revenue growth
to accelerate over the coming three years to an annual compound
rate of over 35%. This ambitious corporate goal will require maximum
productivity and effectiveness from all employees, both current and
prospective. OAISYS's management requested an analysis of its current
personnel structure focused on the alignment of individual employee
motivation with its corporate goal.

Background on Current Human Resources Program   **2**

OAISYS is currently structured departmentally by function. It has
teams for research and development, sales, marketing, operations, and
administration. Every employee has access to the same employment

**[The writer uses the next section to present evidence from
research studies and from interviews with employees.]**

1 Introduction presents problem to be discussed and
establishes scope of report. **2** Heading announces purpose
of section.

Employee Motivation 5

Doug Ames, manager of operations for OAISYS, noted that some of
these issues keep the company from outperforming expectations:
"Communication is not timely or uniform, expectations are not
clear and consistent, and some employees do not contribute
significantly yet nothing is done" (personal communication,
February 28, 2006).

1 Recommendations

It appears that a combination of steps can be used to unlock
greater performance for OAISYS. Most important, steps can be
taken to strengthen the corporate culture in key areas such as
communication, accountability, and appreciation. Employee
feedback indicates that these are areas of weakness or motivators
2 that can be improved. This feedback is summarized in Figure 1.

A plan to use communication effectively to set expectations,
share results in a timely fashion, and publicly offer appreciation
to specific contributors will likely go a long way toward aligning
individual motivation with corporate goals. Additionally, holding
individuals accountable for results will bring parity to the
workplace.

3

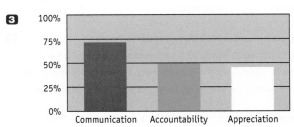

4 *Figure 1.* Areas of greatest need for improvements in motivation.

1 Writer presents recommendations based on his research
and interviews. **2** Figure summarizes research findings.
3 Figure graphically illustrates support for key
recommendation. **4** Figure number and caption appear
below figure.

12j Professional memo (business)

For a course in business writing, Kelly Ratajczak wrote a proposal, in the form of a memorandum. Her purpose was to persuade her supervisor of the benefits of a wellness program for employees at the medium-size company where she was an intern.

Professional memo   **First page**

MEMORANDUM   **1**

To: Jay Crosson, Senior Vice President, Human Resources   **2**

From: Kelly Ratajczak, Intern, Purchasing Department

Subject: Proposal to Add a Wellness Program

Date: April 24, 2011

Health care costs are rising. In the long run, implementing   **3**
a wellness program in our corporate culture will decrease the
company's health care costs.

                                                         4

Research indicates that nearly 70% of health care costs are from   **5**
common illnesses related to high blood pressure, overweight, lack
of exercise, high cholesterol, stress, poor nutrition, and other
preventable health issues (Hall, 2006). Health care costs are a
major expense for most businesses, and they do not reflect costs
due to the loss of productivity or absenteeism. A wellness program
would address most, if not all of these health care issues and
related costs.

Benefits of Healthier Employees   **6**

Not only would a wellness program substantially reduce costs associated
with employee health care, but our company would prosper through

---

1 Formatting consistent with typical style for business memo.
2 First page counted in numbering, but no page number
appears. **3** Clear point in first paragraph. **4** Paragraphs
separated by extra line of space; first line of paragraph not
indented. **5** Introduction provides background information.
6 Headings, flush left and boldface, define sections.

(Annotations indicate business-style formatting and effective
writing.)

12k Social issue paper (composition)

Sophie Harba, a student in a composition class, wrote the following social issue paper on the government's role in legislating food choices. Harba's paper is documented with in-text citations and a list of references in APA style. Her instructor did not require an abstract for this brief paper.

Social issue paper   **Title page**

1 Running head: PERSONAL CHOICES VS. PUBLIC HEALTH   1 **2**

3   What's for Dinner?
                Personal Choices vs. Public Health
                      Sophie Harba
                    Middleboro College

4   Author Note
        This paper was prepared for English 1101, taught by
Professor Baros-Moon.

1 Short title, no more than 50 characters, in all capital letters on all pages; words "Running head" and colon on title page only. **2** Arabic page number on all pages. **3** Full title and writer's name and affiliation, centered. **4** Author's note (optional) for extra information.

(Annotations indicate APA-style formatting and effective writing.)

Social issue paper   **First text page**

PERSONAL CHOICES VS. PUBLIC HEALTH   2 **❶**

What's for Dinner?   **❷**

Personal Choices vs. Public Health

Should the government enact laws to regulate healthy eating   **❸**
choices? Many Americans would answer an emphatic "No," arguing
that what and how much we eat should be left to individual choice
rather than unreasonable laws. Others might argue that it would
be unreasonable for the government not to enact legislation,
given the rise of chronic diseases that result from harmful diets.
In this debate, both the definition of reasonable regulations and
the role of government to legislate food choices are at stake. In   **❹**
the name of public health and safety, state governments have the
responsibility to shape health policies and to regulate healthy
eating choices, especially since doing so offers a potentially large
social benefit for a relatively small cost.

Debates surrounding the government's role in regulating food
have a long history in the United States. According to Goodwin   **❺**
(2006), 19th-century reformers who sought to purify the food
supply were called "fanatics" and "radicals" by critics who argued
that consumers should be free to buy and eat what they want
(p. 77). Thanks to regulations, though, such as the 1906 federal   **❻**
Pure Food and Drug Act, food, beverages, and medicine are largely
free from toxins. In addition, to prevent contamination and the
spread of disease, meat and dairy products are now inspected by
government agents to ensure that they meet health requirements.
Such regulations can be considered reasonable because they   **❼**
protect us from harm with little, if any, noticeable consumer cost.
It is not considered an unreasonable infringement on personal
choice that contaminated meat or arsenic-laced cough drops are
unavailable at our local supermarket. Rather, it is an

❶ Short title, no more than 50 characters, flush left. Page
number, flush right. **❷** Full title, centered and not boldface.
❸ Introduction poses a question. **❹** Thesis presents writer's
main point. **❺** Signal phrase names author. **❻** Parenthetical
citation includes page number. **❼** Writer explains use of a
key term (*reasonable*).

Social issue paper   **Text page**

PERSONAL CHOICES VS. PUBLIC HEALTH   3

important government function to stop such harmful items from
entering the marketplace.

 Even though our food meets current safety standards, there
is a need for further regulation. Not all food dangers, for example,
arise from obvious toxins like arsenic and *E. coli*. A diet that is low
in nutritional value and high in sugars, fats, and refined grains—
grains that have been processed to increase shelf life but that
contain little fiber, iron, and B vitamins—can be damaging over
time (United States, Department of Agriculture and Department
of Health and Human Services, 2010, p. 36). Figure 1 provides a
visual representation of the American diet and how far off it is
from the recommended nutritional standards.

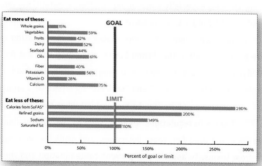

Figure 1. Intake as a percent of recommended nutritional goals
and limits among Americans, by food group. From United States,
Department of Agriculture and Department of Health and Human
Services, 2010, Figure 5-1.

1 Transition guides readers. **2** Figure reinforces writer's
argument with data. **3** Figure number, caption, and source
information.

Social issue paper   **Text page**

PERSONAL CHOICES VS. PUBLIC HEALTH   4

Pollan (2010), who has written extensively about Americans'
unhealthy eating habits, noted that "the Centers for Disease Control
estimates that fully three quarters of US health care spending
goes to treat chronic diseases, most of which are preventable and
linked to diet: heart disease, stroke, type 2 diabetes, and at least a
third of all cancers" ("Food Politics," para. 7). In fact, the amount   **1**
of money the United States spends to treat chronic illnesses is
increasing so rapidly that the Centers for Disease Control labeled
chronic disease "the public health challenge of the 21st century"
(United States, Department of Health and Human Services, 2009,
p. 1). In fighting this epidemic, the primary challenge is not the
need to find a cure; the challenge is to prevent chronic diseases
from striking in the first place.

Legislation, however, is not a popular solution when it
comes to most Americans and the food they eat. According to a   **2**
nationwide poll, 75% of Americans are opposed to laws that restrict
or put limitations on access to unhealthy foods (Neergaard &
Agiesta, 2013). When New York mayor Michael Bloomberg proposed
a regulation in 2012 banning the sale of soft drinks in servings
greater than 12 ounces in restaurants and movie theaters, he was
ridiculed as "Nanny Bloomberg." In California in 2011, legislators
failed to pass a law that would impose a penny-per-ounce tax on
soda, which would have funded obesity prevention programs. And in
Mississippi, legislators passed "a ban on bans—a law that forbids . . .
local restrictions on food or drink" (Conly, 2013, p. A23).

Why is the public largely resistant to laws that would limit
unhealthy choices or penalize those choices with so-called fat
taxes? Many consumers and civil rights advocates find such laws to   **3**
be an unreasonable restriction on individual freedom of choice.

---

1 This web source has no page numbers, but it has section
titles. The citation includes the section title and the paragraph
in that section. **2** Writer treats both sides fairly. **3** Writer
counters opposing views.

Social issue paper   **Text page**

PERSONAL CHOICES VS. PUBLIC HEALTH   5

As Mello, Studdert, and Brennan (2006) pointed out, opposition to food
and beverage regulation is similar to the opposition to early tobacco
legislation: The public views the issue as one of personal responsibility
rather than one requiring government intervention (p. 2602). In other
words, if a person eats unhealthy food and becomes ill as a result,
that is his or her choice. But those who favor legislation claim that
freedom of choice is a myth because of the strong influence of food and
beverage industry marketing on consumers' dietary habits. According
to one nonprofit health advocacy group, food and beverage companies
spend roughly two billion dollars per year marketing directly to children.
As a result, kids see nearly 4,000 ads per year encouraging them to

1 eat unhealthy food and drinks ("Facts," n.d.). As was the case with
antismoking laws passed in recent decades, taxes and legal restrictions on
junk food sales could help to counter the strong marketing messages that
promote unhealthy products.

The United States has a history of state and local public health
laws that have successfully promoted a particular behavior by punishing
an undesirable behavior. The decline in tobacco use as a result of
antismoking taxes and laws is perhaps the most obvious example.
Another example is legislation requiring the use of seat belts, which
have significantly reduced fatalities in car crashes. The U.S. Department
of Transportation (2010) reported that seat belt use saved an average of
more than 14,000 lives per year in the United States between 2000 and
2010 (p. 231). Perhaps seat belt laws have public support because the
cost of wearing a seat belt is small, especially when compared with the
benefit of saving 14,000 lives per year.

Laws designed to prevent chronic disease by promoting
healthier food and beverage consumption also have potentially

2 enormous benefits. To give just one example, Nestle (2013)

1 For a source with no author and date, a short form of
the the title and the abbreviation "n.d." are used in the citation.
2 Writer introduces direct quotation with signal phrase.

Social issue paper   **Text page**

PERSONAL CHOICES VS. PUBLIC HEALTH   6

noted that "a 1% reduction in intake of saturated fat across the
population would prevent more than 30,000 cases of coronary
heart disease annually and save more than a billion dollars in
health care costs" (p. 7). Few would argue that saving lives and
dollars is not an enormous benefit. But three-quarters of Americans
say they would object to the costs needed to achieve this
benefit—the regulations needed to reduce saturated fat intake.

   Why do so many Americans believe there is a degree of personal
choice lost when regulations such as taxes, bans, or portion limits
on unhealthy foods are proposed? Some critics of anti-junk-food laws
believe that even if state and local laws were successful in curbing
chronic diseases, they would still be unacceptable. Resnik (2010)
emphasized that such policies, despite their potential to make our
society healthier, "open the door to excessive government control
over food, which could restrict dietary choices, interfere with cultural,
ethnic, and religious traditions, and exacerbate socioeconomic
inequalities" (p. 31). Resnik acknowledged that his argument relies
on "slippery slope" thinking, but he insists that "social and political
pressures" regarding food regulation make his concerns valid (p. 31).
Yet the social and political pressures that Resnik cited are really just
the desire to improve public health, and limiting access to unhealthy,
artificial ingredients seems a small price to pay. As Gostin and Gostin
(2009) explained, "Interventions that do not pose a truly significant
burden on individual liberty" are justified if they "go a long way towards
safeguarding the health and well-being of the populace" (p. 214).

   To improve public health, advocates such as Bowdoin
College philosophy professor Sarah Conly contend that it is the
government's duty to prevent people from making harmful choices
whenever feasible and whenever public benefits outweigh the
costs. In response to critics who claim that laws aimed at stopping **1**
us from eating whatever we want are an assault on our freedom of
choice, Conly (2013) offered a persuasive counterargument:

1 Long quotation introduced with signal phrase.

12k

Social issue paper	Text page

PERSONAL CHOICES VS. PUBLIC HEALTH 7

1 Laws aren't designed for each one of us individually. Some of us can drive safely at 90 miles per hour, but we're bound by the same laws as the people who can't, because individual speeding laws aren't practical. Giving up a little liberty is something we agree to when we agree to live in a democratic society that is governed by laws. (p. A23)

2 As Conly suggested, we need to change our either/or thinking (either we have complete freedom of choice or we have government regulations and lose our freedom) and instead need to see health as a matter of public good, not individual liberty. Proposals such as Mayor Bloomberg's that seek to limit portions of unhealthy beverages aren't about giving up liberty; they are about asking individuals to choose substantial public health benefits at a very small cost.

3 Despite arguments in favor of regulating unhealthy food as a means to improve public health, public opposition has stood in the way of legislation. Americans freely eat as much unhealthy food as they want, and manufacturers and sellers of these foods have nearly unlimited freedom to promote such products and drive increased consumption, without any requirements to warn the public of potential hazards. Yet mounting scientific evidence points to unhealthy food as a significant contributing factor to chronic disease, which we know is straining our health care system, decreasing Americans' quality of life, and leading to unnecessary premature deaths. Americans must consider whether to allow the costly trend of rising chronic disease to continue in the name of personal choice or whether to support the regulatory changes and public health policies that will reverse that trend.

1 Long quotation indented with no quotation marks.
2 Writer connects quotation to her argument. **3** Conclusion sums up argument.

Social issue paper   **Reference list (partial)**

PERSONAL CHOICES VS. PUBLIC HEALTH   8

References   **1**

Conly, S. (2013, March 25). Three cheers for the nanny state. *The*   **2**
     New York Times, p. A23.

The facts on junk food marketing and kids. (n.d.). Retrieved from   **3**
     Prevention Institute website: www.preventioninstitute.org
     /focus-areas/supporting-healthy-food-a-activity/supporting
     -healthy-food-and-activity-environments-advocacy
     /get-involved-were-not-buying-it/735-were-not-buying-it-the
     -facts-on-junk-food-marketing-and-kids.html

Goodwin, L. S. (2006). *The pure food, drink, and drug crusaders,*   **4**
     1879-1914. Jefferson, NC: McFarland.

Gostin, L. O., & Gostin, K. G. (2009). A broader liberty: J. S. Mill,
     paternalism, and the public's health. *Public Health, 123*(3),
     214-221. https://doi.org/10.1016/j.puhe.2008.12.024

Mello, M. M., Studdert, D. M., & Brennan, T. A. (2006). Obesity—   **5**
     The new frontier of public health law. *The New England*
     Journal of Medicine, 354(24), 2601-2610. https://doi
     .org/10.1056/NEJMhpr060227

Neergaard, L., & Agiesta, J. (2013, January 4). Obesity's a crisis
     but we want our junk food, poll shows. *The Huffington Post*.
     Retrieved from https://www.huffingtonpost.com

Nestle, M. (2013). *Food politics: How the food industry influences*
     nutrition and health. Berkeley, CA: University of California Press.

Pollan, M. (2010, June 10). The food movement, rising. *The*
     New York Review of Books. Retrieved from http://www
     .nybooks.com

Resnik, D. (2010). Trans fat bans and human freedom. *The American*
     Journal of Bioethics, 10(3), 27-32.

1 List of references on new page; heading centered and
not boldface. **2** List alphabetized by authors' last names,
government organization names, or titles (for works with
no authors). Authors' names inverted, with initial(s) for first
names. **3** Source with unknown author alphabetized by first
word in title (excluding article *the*). Because publication date
is unknown, "(n.d.)" is used. **4** Double-spaced throughout.
First line of each entry flush left; subsequent lines indented
½". **5** For a work with up to seven authors, all authors'
names are listed; ampersand (&) precedes last author's name.

Documenting Sources in APA Style

Directory to APA in-text citation models

The APA system for documenting sources is set forth in the *Publication Manual of the American Psychological Association,* 6th ed. (Washington, DC: APA, 2010).

13 APA in-text citations

APA's in-text citations provide the author's last name and the year of publication, usually before the cited material, and a page number in parentheses directly after the cited material. In the following models, the elements of the in-text citation are highlighted.

NOTE: APA style requires the use of the past tense or the present perfect tense in signal phrases introducing cited material: *Smith (2012) reported, Smith (2012) has argued.* See also section 9b.

● **1. Basic format for a quotation**   Ordinarily, introduce the quotation with a signal phrase that includes the author's last name followed by the year of publication in parentheses. Put the page number (preceded by "p.") in parentheses after the quotation. For sources from the web without page numbers, see item 12a.

Çubukçu (2012) argued that for a student-centered approach to work, students must maintain "ownership for their goals and activities" (p. 64).

If the author is not named in the signal phrase, place the author's name, the year, and the page number in parentheses after the quotation: (Çubukçu, 2012, p. 64). (See items 6 and 12 for citing sources that lack authors; item 12 also explains how to handle sources without dates or page numbers.)

NOTE: Do not include a month in an in-text citation, even if the entry in the reference list includes the month.

● **2. Basic format for a summary or a paraphrase**   As for a quotation (see item 1), include the author's last name and the year either in a signal phrase introducing the material or in parentheses following it. Use a page number, if one is available, following the cited material. For sources from the web without page numbers, see item 12a.

Watson (2008) offered a case study of the Cincinnati Public Schools Virtual High School, in which students were able to engage in highly individualized instruction according to their own needs, strengths, and learning styles, using 10 teachers as support (p. 7).

The Cincinnati Public Schools Virtual High School brought students together to engage in highly individualized instruction according to their own needs, strengths, and learning styles, using 10 teachers as support (Watson, 2008, p. 7).

● **3. Work with two authors**   Name both authors in the signal phrase or in parentheses each time you cite the work. In the parentheses, use "&" between the authors' names; in the signal phrase, use "and."

According to Donitsa-Schmidt and Zuzovsky (2014), "demographic growth in the school population" can lead to teacher shortages (p. 426).

In the United States, most public school systems are struggling with teacher shortages, which are projected to worsen as the number of applicants to education schools decreases (Donitsa-Schmidt & Zuzovsky, 2014, p. 420).

● **4. Work with three to five authors** Identify all authors in the signal phrase or in parentheses the first time you cite the source.

In 2013, Harper, Findlen, Ibori, and Wenz studied teachers' perceptions of project-based learning (PBL) before and after participating in a PBL pilot program.

In subsequent citations, use the first author's name followed by "et al." in either the signal phrase or the parentheses.

Surprisingly, Harper et al. (2013) advised school administrators "not to jump into project-based pedagogy without training and feedback."

● **5. Work with six or more authors** Use the first author's name followed by "et al." in the signal phrase or in parentheses.

Hermann et al. (2012) tracked 42 students over a three-year period to look closely at the performance of students in the laptop program (p. 49).

● **6. Work with unknown author** If the author is unknown, mention the work's title in the signal phrase or give the first word or two of the title in the parentheses. Titles of short works such as articles are put in quotation marks; titles of long works such as books and reports are italicized.

Collaboration increases significantly among students who own or have regular access to a laptop ("Tech Seeds," 2015).

NOTE: In the rare case when "Anonymous" is specified as the author, treat it as if it were a real name: (Anonymous, 2011). In the list of references, also use Anonymous as the author's name.

● **7. Organization as author** Name the organization in the signal phrase or in the parentheses the first time you cite the source.

According to the International Society for Technology in Education (2016), "Student-centered learning moves students from passive receivers of information to active participants in their own discovery process."

If the organization has a familiar abbreviation, you may include it in brackets the first time you cite the source and use the abbreviation alone in later citations.

FIRST CITATION   (Texas Higher Education Coordinating Board [THECB], 2012)

LATER CITATIONS   (THECB, 2012)

● **8. Authors with the same last name**   If your reference list includes two or more authors with the same last name, use initials with the last names in your in-text citations.

Research by E. Smith (1989) revealed that . . .

One 2012 study contradicted . . . (R. Smith, p. 234).

● **9. Two or more works by the same author in the same year**   In the reference list, you will use lowercase letters ("a," "b," and so on) with the year to order the entries. (See item 8 on p. 119.) Use those same letters with the year in the in-text citation.

Research by Durgin (2013b) has yielded new findings about the role of smartphones in the classroom.

● **10. Two or more works in the same parentheses**   Put the works in the same order in which they appear in the reference list, separated with semicolons.

Researchers have indicated that studies of educational technology initiatives reveal the high cost of change (Nazer, 2015; Serrao et al., 2014).

● **11. Multiple citations to the same work in one paragraph** If you give the author's name in the text of your paper (not in parentheses) and you mention that source again in the text of the same paragraph, give only the author's name, not the date, in the later citation. If any subsequent reference in the same paragraph is in parentheses, include both the author and the date in the parentheses.

Principal Jean Patrice said, "You have to be able to reach students where they are instead of making them come to you. If you don't, you'll lose them" (personal communication, April 10, 2006). Patrice expressed her desire to see all students get something out of their educational experience. This feeling is common among members of Waverly's faculty. With such a positive view of student potential, it is no wonder that 97% of Waverly High School graduates go on to a four-year university (Patrice, 2006).

● **12. Web source**   Cite sources from the web as you would cite any other source, giving the author and the year when they are available.

Atkinson (2011) found that children who spent at least four hours a day engaged in online activities in an academic environment were less likely to want to play video games or watch TV after school.

Usually a page number is not available; occasionally a web source will lack an author or a date (see 12a, 12b, and 12c).

a. No page numbers   When a web source lacks stable numbered pages, you may include paragraph numbers or headings to help readers locate the passage being cited.

If the source has numbered paragraphs, use the paragraph number preceded by the abbreviation "para." (or "paras." for more than one paragraph): (Hall, 2012, para. 5). If the source has no numbered paragraphs but contains headings, cite the appropriate heading in parentheses.

Crush and Jayasingh (2015) pointed out that several other school districts in low-income areas had "jump-started their distance learning initiatives with available grant funds" ("Funding Change," para. 6).

b. Unknown author   If no author is named in the source, mention the title of the source in a signal phrase or give the first word or two of the title in parentheses (see also item 6). (If an organization serves as the author, see item 7.)

A student's IEP may, in fact, recommend the use of mobile technology ("Considerations," 2012).

c. Unknown date   When the source does not give a date, use the abbreviation "n.d." (for "no date").

Administrators believe 1-to-1 programs boost learner engagement (Magnus, n.d.).

● **13. An entire website**   If you are citing an entire website, not an internal page or a section, give the URL in the text of your paper but do not include it in the reference list.

The Berkeley Center for Teaching and Learning website (https://teaching.berkeley.edu/) shares ideas for using mobile technology in the classroom.

● **14. Multivolume work**   If you have used more than one volume from a multivolume work, add the volume number in parentheses with the page number.

Banford (2013) has demonstrated steady increases in performance since the program began a decade ago (Vol. 2, p. 135).

● **15. Personal communication**   Interviews that you conduct, memos, letters, email messages, social media posts, and similar communications that would be difficult for your readers to retrieve should be cited in the text only, not in the reference list. (Use the source's first initial as well as the last name in parentheses.)

One of Yim's colleagues, who has studied the effect of social media on children's academic progress, has contended that the benefits of this technology for children under 12 years old are few (F. Johnson, personal communication, October 20, 2013).

● **16. Course materials**   Cite lecture notes from your instructor or your own class notes as personal communication (see item 15). If your instructor's material contains publication information, cite as you would the appropriate source. See also item 62 on page 137.

● **17. Part of a source (chapter, figure)**   To cite a specific part of a source, such as a whole chapter or a figure or table, identify the element in parentheses. Don't abbreviate terms such as "Figure," "Chapter," and "Section"; "page" is abbreviated "p." (or "pp." for more than one page).

The data support the finding that peer relationships are difficult to replicate in a completely online environment (Hanniman, 2010, Figure 8-3, p. 345).

● **18. Indirect source (source quoted in another source)** When a writer's or a speaker's quoted words appear in a source written by someone else, begin the parenthetical citation with the words "as cited in." In the following example, Demski is the author of the source in the reference list; that source contains a quotation by Cator.

Karen Cator, director of the U.S. Department of Education's Office of Educational Technology, calls technology "the essence" of a personalized learning environment (as cited in Demski, 2012, p. 34).

● **19. Sacred or classical text** Identify the text, the version or edition you used, and the relevant part (chapter, verse, line). It is not necessary to include the source in the reference list.

Peace activists have long cited the biblical prophet's vision of a world without war: "And they shall beat their swords into plowshares, and their spears into pruning hooks; nation shall not lift up sword against nation, neither shall they learn war any more" (Isaiah 2:4 Revised Standard Version).

14 APA list of references

The information you will need for the reference list at the end of your paper will differ slightly for some sources, but the main principles apply to all sources: You should identify an author, a creator, or a producer whenever possible; give a title; and provide the date on which the source was produced. Some sources will require page numbers; some will require a publisher; and some will require retrieval information.

▶ Directory to APA reference list models, **p. 114**
▶ General guidelines for the reference list, **p. 116**

Directory to APA reference list models

BOOKS AND OTHER LONG WORKS (*CONTINUED*)

WEBSITES AND PARTS OF WEBSITES

AUDIO, VISUAL, AND MULTIMEDIA SOURCES

PERSONAL COMMUNICATION AND SOCIAL MEDIA

General guidelines for the reference list

In the list of references, include only sources that you have quoted, summarized, or paraphrased in your paper.

Authors and dates

- Alphabetize entries by authors' last names; if a work has no author, alphabetize it by its title.
- For all authors' names, put the last name first, followed by a comma; use initials for the first and middle names.
- With two or more authors, use an ampersand (&) before the last author's name. Separate the names with commas. Include names for the first seven authors; if there are eight or more authors, give the first six authors, three ellipsis dots, and the last author.
- If the author is a company or an organization, give the name in normal order.
- Put the date of publication in parentheses immediately after the first element of the citation.
- For books, give the year of publication. For magazines, newspapers, and newsletters, give the year and month or the year, month, and day. For web sources, give the date of posting, if available. Use the season if a publication gives only a season, not a month.

Titles

- Italicize the titles and subtitles of books, journals, and other long works. If a book title contains another book title or an article title, do not italicize the internal title and do not put quotation marks around it.
- Use no italics or quotation marks for the titles of articles. If an article title contains another article title or a term usually placed in quotation marks, use quotation marks around the internal title or the term.
- For books and articles, capitalize only the first word of the title and subtitle and all proper nouns.
- For the titles of journals, magazines, and newspapers, capitalize all words of four letters or more (and all nouns, pronouns, verbs, adjectives, and adverbs of any length).

Place of publication and publisher

- Take the information about a book from its title page and copyright page. If more than one place of publication is listed, use only the first.

- Give the city and state for all US cities. Use postal abbreviations for all states.

- Give the city and country for all non-US cities; include the province for Canadian cities. Do not abbreviate the country and province.

- Do not give a state if the publisher's name includes it (Ann Arbor: University of Michigan Press, for example).

- In publishers' names, omit terms such as "Company" (or "Co.") and "Inc." but keep "Books" and "Press." Omit first names or initials (Norton, not W. W. Norton).

- If the publisher is the same as the author, use the word "Author" in the publisher position.

Volume, issue, and page numbers

- For a journal or a magazine, give only the volume number if the publication is paginated continuously through each volume; give the volume and issue numbers if each issue begins on page 1.

- Italicize the volume number and put the issue number, not italicized, in parentheses.

- When an article appears on consecutive pages, provide the range of pages. When an article does not appear on consecutive pages, give all page numbers: A1, A17.

- For daily and weekly newspapers, use "p." or "pp." before page numbers (if any). For journals and magazines, do not use "p." or "pp."

URLs, DOIs, and other retrieval information

- For articles and books from the web, use the DOI (digital object identifier) if the source has one, and do not give a URL. If a source does not have a DOI, give the URL.

- Use a retrieval date for a web source only if the content is likely to change. Most of the examples in this section do not show a retrieval date because the content of the sources is stable. If you are unsure about whether to use a date, include it or consult your instructor.

14a General guidelines for listing authors

The formatting of authors' names in items 1–11 applies to all sources in print and on the web—books, articles, websites, and so on. For more models of specific source types, see items 12–65.

● **1. Single author**

author: last name + initial(s)   year (book   title (book)

Rosenberg, T. (2011). *Join the club: How peer pressure can*

place of publication   publisher

transform the world. New York, NY: Norton.

● **2. Two to seven authors** List up to seven authors by last names followed by initials. Use an ampersand (&) before the name of the last author. (See items 3–5 on pp. 108–109 for in-text citations.)

all authors: last name + initial(s)   year (journal)   title (article)

Kim, E. H., Hollon, S. D., & Olatunji, B. O. (2016). Clinical errors

journal title   volume   page(s)

in cognitive-behavior therapy. *Psychotherapy, 53,* 325–330.

DOI

https://doi.org/10.1037/pst0000074

● **3. Eight or more authors** List the first six authors followed by three ellipsis dots and the last author's name.

Tøttrup, A. P., Klaassen, R. H. G., Kristensen, M. W., Strandberg, R., Vardanis, Y., Lindström, Å., . . . Thorup, K. (2012). Drought in Africa caused delayed arrival of European songbirds. *Science, 338,* 1307. https://doi.org/10.1126 /science.1227548

● **4. Organization as author**

author: organization name   year   title (book)

American Psychiatric Association. (2013). *Diagnostic and statistical*

edition   place of publication   organization as author and publisher

manual of mental disorders (5th ed.). Washington, DC: Author.

● **5. Unknown author**

title (article) | year + month + day (weekly publication) | journal title

The rise of the sharing economy. (2013, March 9). *The Economist,*

volume, issue | page(s)

406(8826), 14.

● **6. Author using a pseudonym (pen name) or screen name** Use the author's real name, if known, and give the pseudonym or screen name in brackets exactly as it appears in the source. If only the screen name is known, begin with that name and do not use brackets. (See also items 44 and 65 on citing screen names in social media.)

screen name | year + month + day (daily publication) | title of original article

littlebigman. (2012, December 13). Re: Who's watching? Privacy

label

concerns persist as smart meters roll out [Comment].

title of publication

National Geographic Daily News. Retrieved from http://news

URL for web publication

.nationalgeographic.com/

● **7. Two or more works by the same author** Use the author's name for all entries. List the entries by year, the earliest first.

Heinrich, B. (2009). *Summer world: A season of bounty.*
New York, NY: Ecco.

Heinrich, B. (2012). *Life everlasting: The animal way of death.*
New York, NY: Houghton Mifflin Harcourt.

● **8. Two or more works by the same author in the same year** List the works alphabetically by title. In the parentheses, following the year add "a," "b," and so on. Use these same letters when giving the year in the in-text citation. (See also item 9 on p. 110.)

Bower, B. (2012a, December 15). Families in flux. *Science News,*
182(12), 16.

Bower, B. (2012b, November 3). Human-Neandertal mating gets
a new date. *Science News, 182*(9), 8.

● **9. Editor** Use the abbreviation "Ed." for one editor, "Eds." for more than one editor.

all editors:
last name + initial(s)   year
Carr, S. C., MacLachlan, M., & Furnham, A. (Eds.). (2012).

                                        place of
              title (book)   publication   publisher
    Humanitarian work psychology. New York, NY: Palgrave.

● **10. Author and editor** Begin with the name of the author, followed by the name of the editor and the abbreviation "Ed." in parentheses. For a book with an author and two or more editors, use the abbreviation "Ed." after each editor's name: Gray, W., & Jones, P. (Ed.), & Smith, A. (Ed.).

author   editor   year   title (book)
James, W., & Pelikan, J. (Ed.). (2009). *The varieties of religious*
                    place of
                    publication   publisher
    experience. New York, NY: Library of America. (Original
            original
    publication information

    work published 1902)

● **11. Translator** Begin with the name of the author and the date. After the title, in parentheses place the name of the translator and the abbreviation "Trans." (for "Translator"). Add the original date of publication at the end of the entry.

author   year   title (book)   translator
Scheffer, P. (2011). *Immigrant nations* (L. Waters, Trans.).
        place of   original
        publication   publisher   publication information
    Cambridge, England: Polity Press. (Original work published

    2007)

14b Articles and other short works

▶ Citation at a glance: Online article in a journal or
    magazine, **p. 123**
▶ Citation at a glance: Article from a database, **p. 124**

● **12. Article in a journal** If an article from the web or a database has no DOI, include the URL for the journal's home page.

a. Print

all authors:
last name + initial(s)   year

Bippus, A. M., Dunbar, N. E., & Liu, S.-J. (2012). Humorous

article title

responses to interpersonal complaints: Effects of humor

journal title

style and nonverbal expression. *The Journal of Psychology,*

volume page(s)

146, 437–453.

b. Web

all authors:
last name + initial(s)   year   article title

Vargas, N., & Schafer, M. H. (2013). Diversity in action:

Interpersonal networks and the distribution of advice.

volume,
journal title   issue   page(s)   DOI

Social Science Research, 42(1), 46–58. https://doi.org

/10.1016/j.ssresearch.2012.08.013

author   year   article title

Brenton, S. (2011). When the personal becomes political:

journal title
(no volume available)

Mitigating damage following scandals. *Current Research in*

URL for journal home page

Social Psychology. Retrieved from https://uiowa.edu/crisp

/crisp/

c. Database

author   year   article title

Sohn, K. (2012). The social class origins of U.S. teachers, 1860-1920.

volume,
journal title   issue   page(s)   DOI

Journal of Social History, 45(4), 908–935. https://doi.org

/10.1093/jsh/shr121

● **13. Article in a magazine** If an article from the web
or a database has no DOI, include the URL for the
magazine's home page.

a. Print

author — year + month (monthly magazine) — article title

Comstock, J. (2012, December). The underrated sense.

magazine title — volume, issue — page(s)

Psychology Today, 45(6), 46–47.

b. Web

author — date of posting (when available) — article title

Burns, J. (2012, December 3). The measure of all things.

magazine title — URL for home page

The American Prospect. Retrieved from http://prospect.org/

c. Database

author — year + month (monthly magazine) — article title — magazine title — volume, issue

Tucker, A. (2012, November). Primal instinct. *Smithsonian, 43*(7),

page(s) — URL for magazine home page

54–63. Retrieved from http://www.smithsonianmag.com/

● **14. Article in a newspaper**

a. Print

author — year + month + day — article title

Swarns, R. L. (2012, December 9). A family, for a few days a year.

newspaper title — page(s)

The New York Times, pp. 1, 20.

b. Web

author: last name + initial(s) — year + month + day

Villanueva-Whitman, E. (2012, November 27). Working to

article title — newspaper title

stimulate memory function. *Des Moines Register.* Retrieved

URL for home page

from http://www.desmoinesregister.com/

● **15. Abstract** Place the label "Abstract" in brackets after the article title.

a. Abstract of a journal article

Morales, J., Calvo, A., & Bialystok, E. (2013). Working memory
development in monolingual and bilingual children
[Abstract]. *Journal of Experimental Child Psychology, 114,*
187-202. Retrieved from http://www.sciencedirect.com/

Citation at a glance

Online article in a journal or magazine APA

To cite an online article in a journal or magazine in APA style, include the following elements:

1 Author(s)
2 Year of publication for journal; complete date for magazine
3 Title and subtitle of article
4 Name of journal or magazine

5 Volume number; issue number, if required (see p. 117)
6 DOI if the article has one; otherwise, URL for journal or magazine home page

ONLINE ARTICLE

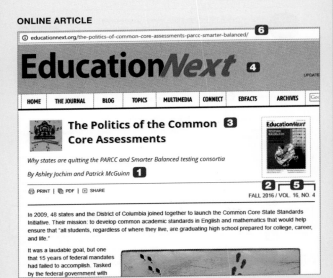

REFERENCE LIST ENTRY FOR AN ONLINE ARTICLE IN A JOURNAL OR MAGAZINE

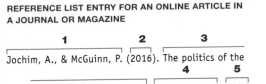

                    1   2   3
Jochim, A., & McGuinn, P. (2016). The politics of the
                                        4   5
        Common Core assessments. *Education Next, 16*(4).
                                6
        Retrieved from educationnext.org/

For more on citing articles in APA style, see items 12–14.

Citation at a glance

Article from a database `APA`

To cite an article from a database in APA style, include the following elements:

1. Author(s)
2. Year of publication for journal; complete date for magazine or newspaper
3. Title and subtitle of article
4. Name of periodical
5. Volume number; issue number, if required (see p. 117)
6. Page number(s)
7. DOI (digital object identifier)
8. URL for periodical's home page (if there is no DOI)

DATABASE RECORD

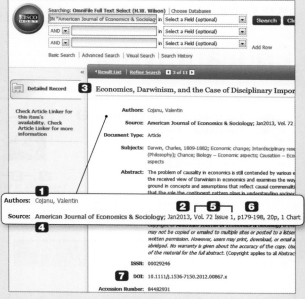

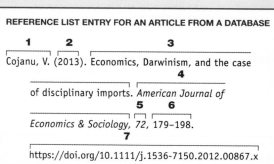

REFERENCE LIST ENTRY FOR AN ARTICLE FROM A DATABASE

Cojanu, V. (2013). Economics, Darwinism, and the case of disciplinary imports. *American Journal of Economics & Sociology, 72,* 179–198.

https://doi.org/10.1111/j.1536-7150.2012.00867.x

(1) (2) (3) (4) (5) (6) (7)

For more on citing articles from a database in APA style, see items 12 and 13.

b. Abstract of a paper

Denham, B. (2012). Diffusing deviant behavior: A communication
     perspective on the construction of moral panics
     [Abstract]. Paper presented at the AEJMC 2012
     Conference, Chicago, IL. Retrieved from http://www.aejmc
     .org/home/2012/04/ctm-2012-abstracts/

● **16. Supplemental material**   Cite as you would an article,
giving the author, date, and title of the supplemental
material. Add the label "Supplemental material" in
brackets following the title.

Reis, S., Grennfelt, P., Klimont, Z., Amann, M., ApSimon, H.,
     Hettelingh, J.-P., . . . Williams, M. (2012). From acid
     rain to climate change [Supplemental material]. *Science,*
     338(6111), 1153–1154. https://doi.org/10.1126
     /science.1226514

● **17. Letter to the editor**   If the letter has no title, use
the bracketed label "Letter to the editor" as the title, as
in the following example.

Lim, C. (2012, November-December). [Letter to the editor].
     Sierra. Retrieved from http://www.sierraclub.org/sierra/

● **18. Editorial or other unsigned article**

The business case for transit dollars [Editorial]. (2012,
     December 9). *Star Tribune.* Retrieved from http://www
     .startribune.com/

● **19. Newsletter article**

Scrivener, L. (n.d.). Why is the minimum wage issue important
     for food justice advocates? *Food Workers—Food Justice, 15.*
     Retrieved from http://www.thedatabank.com/dpg/199
     /pm.asp?nav=1&ID=41429

● **20. Review**   In brackets, give the type of work
reviewed, the title, and the author for a book or the
year for a film. If the review has no author or title, use
the material in brackets as the title.

Aviram, R. B. (2012). [Review of the book *What do I say?*
     The therapist's guide to answering client questions, by
     L. N. Edelstein & C. A. Waehler]. *Psychotherapy, 49*(4),
     570-571. https://doi.org/10.1037/a0029815

Bradley, A., & Olufs, E. (2012). Family dynamics and school
violence [Review of the motion picture *We need to talk about
Kevin*, 2011]. *PsycCRITIQUES, 57*(49). https://doi.org/10
.1037/a0030982

● **21. Published interview**

Githongo, J. (2012, November 20). A conversation with John
Githongo [Interview by Baobab]. *The Economist*. Retrieved
from http://www.economist.com/

● **22. Article in a reference work (encyclopedia, dictionary, wiki)**

a. Print

Konijn, E. A. (2008). Affects and media exposure. In W. Donsbach
(Ed.), *The international encyclopedia of communication*
(Vol. 1, pp. 123–129). Malden, MA: Blackwell.

b. Web

Ethnomethodology. (2006). In *STS wiki*. Retrieved December
15, 2012, from http://www.stswiki.org/index.php?title
=Ethnomethodology

● **23. Comment on an online article**   If the writer's real
name and screen name are given, put the real name
first, followed by the screen name in brackets.

Danboy125. (2012, November 9). Re: No flowers on the psych
ward [Comment]. *The Atlantic*. Retrieved from http://www
.theatlantic.com/

● **24. Testimony before a legislative body**

Carmona, R. H. (2004, March 2). *The growing epidemic of
childhood obesity*. Testimony before the Subcommittee
on Competition, Foreign Commerce, and Infrastructure of
the U.S. Senate Committee on Commerce, Science, and
Transportation. Retrieved from http://www.hhs.gov/asl
/testify/t040302.html

● **25. Paper presented at a meeting or symposium (unpublished)**

Karimi, S., Key, G., & Tat, D. (2011, April 22). *Complex
predicates in focus*. Paper presented at the West Coast
Conference on Formal Linguistics, Tucson, AZ.

● **26. Poster session at a conference**

Lacara, N. (2011, April 24). *Predicate which appositives*. Poster
session presented at the West Coast Conference on Formal
Linguistics, Tucson, AZ.

14c Books and other long works

▶ Citation at a glance: Book, **p. 128**

● **27. Basic format for a book**

a. Print

author(s):
last name
+ initial(s)   year   book title

Child, B. J. (2012). *Holding our world together: Ojibwe women*
                                         place of
                                         publication publisher
and the survival of community. New York, NY: Viking.

b. Web (or online library) Give the URL for the home page
of the website or the online library.

author(s)   year   book title

Amponsah, N. A., & Falola, T. (2012). *Women's roles in sub-*
                                              URL
Saharan Africa. Retrieved from http://books.google.com/

c. E-book Give the version in brackets after the title
("Kindle version," "Nook version," and so on). Include
the DOI or, if a DOI is not available, the URL for the home
page of the site from which you downloaded the book.

Wolf, D. A., & Folbre, N. (Eds.). (2012). *Universal coverage of
long-term care in the United States* [Adobe Digital Editions
version]. Retrieved from https://www.russellsage.org/

d. Database Give the URL for the database.

Beasley, M. H. (2012). *Women of the Washington press: Politics,
prejudice, and persistence*. Retrieved from http://muse.jhu.edu/

● **28. Edition other than the first**

Harvey, P. (2013). *An introduction to Buddhism: Teachings,
history, and practices* (2nd ed.). Cambridge, England:
Cambridge University Press.

Citation at a glance
Book APA

To cite a print book in APA style, include the following elements:

1 Author(s)
2 Year of publication
3 Title and subtitle
4 Place of publication
5 Publisher

TITLE PAGE

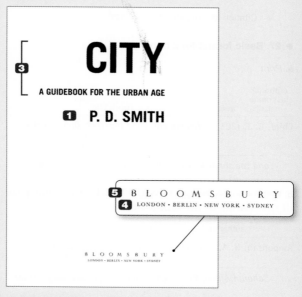

3 **CITY**
A GUIDEBOOK FOR THE URBAN AGE

1 **P. D. SMITH**

5 BLOOMSBURY
4 LONDON · BERLIN · NEW YORK · SYDNEY

BLOOMSBURY
LONDON · BERLIN · NEW YORK · SYDNEY

FROM COPYRIGHT PAGE

First published in Great Britain and the USA in 2012 2

Bloomsbury Publishing Plc, 50 Bedford Square, London WC1B 3DP
Bloomsbury USA, 175 Fifth Avenue, New York, NY 10010

Copyright © 2012 by P. D. Smith

REFERENCE LIST ENTRY FOR A PRINT BOOK

1   2   3
Smith, P. D. (2012). *City: A guidebook for the urban age.*
        4   5
London, England: Bloomsbury.

For more on citing books in APA style, see items 27–34.

● **29. Selection in an anthology or a collection**

a. Entire anthology

editor(s)   year

Warren, A. E. A., Lerner, R. M., & Phelps, E. (Eds.). (2012).

title of anthology

Thriving and spirituality among youth: Research perspectives

place of
publication publisher

and future possibilities. Hoboken, NJ: Wiley.

b. Selection in an anthology

author of
selection   year   title of selection

Lazar, S. W. (2012). Neural correlates of positive youth development.

editors of anthology

In A. E. A. Warren, R. M. Lerner, & E. Phelps (Eds.), *Thriving*

title of anthology

and spirituality among youth: Research perspectives and

page numbers   place of
of selection   publication publisher

future possibilities (pp. 77–90). Hoboken, NJ: Wiley.

● **30. Multivolume work**

a. All volumes

Khalakdina, M. (2008–2011). *Human development in the Indian
    context: A socio-cultural focus* (Vols. 1–2). New Delhi,
    India: Sage.

b. One volume, with title

Jensen, R. E. (Ed.). (2012). *Voices of the American West: Vol. 1.
    The Indian interviews of Eli S. Ricker, 1903-1919.* Lincoln:
    University of Nebraska Press.

● **31. Introduction, preface, foreword, or afterword**

Zachary, L. J. (2012). Foreword. In L. A. Daloz, *Mentor: Guiding
    the journey of adult learners* (pp. v–vii). San Francisco, CA:
    Jossey-Bass.

● **32. Dictionary or other reference work**

Leong, F. T. L. (Ed.). (2008). *Encyclopedia of counseling*
    (Vols. 1–4). Thousand Oaks, CA: Sage.

● 33. Republished book

Mailer, N. (2008). *Miami and the siege of Chicago: An informal
    history of the Republican and Democratic conventions of
    1968*. New York, NY: New York Review Books. (Original
    work published 1968)

● 34. Book in a language other than English   Place the
English translation, not italicized, in brackets.

Carminati, G. G., & Méndez, A. (2012). *Étapes de vie, étapes
    de soins* [Stages of life, stages of care]. Chêne-Bourg,
    Switzerland: Médecine & Hygiène.

● 35. Dissertation

a. Published

Hymel, K. M. (2009). *Essays in urban economics* (Doctoral
    dissertation). Available from ProQuest Dissertations and
    Theses database. (AAT 3355930)

b. Unpublished

Mitchell, R. D. (2007). *The Wesleyan Quadrilateral: Relocating
    the conversation* (Unpublished doctoral dissertation).
    Claremont School of Theology, Claremont, CA.

● 36. Conference proceedings

Yu, F.-Y., Hirashima, T., Supnithi, T., & Biswas, G. (2011).
    *Proceedings of the 19th International Conference on
    Computers in Education: ICCE 2011*. Retrieved from http://
    www.apsce.net:8080/icce2011/program/proceedings/

● 37. Government document   If the document has a
report number, place the number in parentheses after
the title. If it does not have a number, place a period
after the title.

U.S. Census Bureau, Bureau of Economic Analysis. (2012,
    December). *U.S. international trade in goods and services,
    October 2012* (Report No. CB12-232, BEA12-55, FT-900
    [12-10]). Retrieved from http://www.census.gov/
    foreign-trade/Press-Release/2012pr/10/

● 38. Report from a private organization   For a print
source, if the publisher and the author are the same,
see item 4 on page 118.

Ford Foundation. (2012, November). *Eastern Africa*. Retrieved
    from http://www.fordfoundation.org/pdfs/library/Eastern
    -Africa-brochure-2012.pdf

● **39. Legal source**   The title of a court case is italicized
in an in-text citation but not in the reference list.

Sweatt v. Painter, 339 U.S. 629 (1950). Retrieved from Cornell
    University Law School, Legal Information Institute
    website: http://www.law.cornell.edu/supct/html/historics
    /USSC_CR_0339_0629_ZS.html

● **40. Sacred or classical text**   It is not necessary to list
sacred works such as the Bible or the Qur'an or classical
Greek and Roman works (such as the *Odyssey*) in your
reference list. See item 19 on page 113 for how to cite
these sources in the text of your paper.

14d Websites and parts of websites

> Citation at a glance: Section in a web document, **p. 132**

● **41. Entire website**   Do not include an entire website
in the reference list. Give the URL in parentheses in the
text of your paper. (See item 13 on p. 112.)

● **42. Document from a website**   If the publisher is known
and is not named as the author, include the publisher in
your retrieval statement. (See models on p. 133.)

Guidelines for citing online sources with incomplete information

When you cite an online source, always include the
following four key pieces of information if you can:
author(s), date, title, and source URL. Sometimes,
you may want to cite an online source that does not
include one or more of these pieces of information. In
such cases, use the following guidelines:

- **Unknown author.** List the title of the article (or the
  name of the website, if there is no title) first. Then
  list the date of publication, if known. Finally, write
  "Retrieved from" followed by the entire source URL.
  (See also item 5 in section 14a.)

- **Unknown publication date.** After the author's
  name — or after the title, if the author is unknown —
  write "(n.d.)."

- **No title.** In place of a title, you may list the name
  of the website or the section heading under which
  the cited information appears.

Citation at a glance
Section in a web document APA

To cite a section in a document in APA style, include the
following elements:

1 Author(s)
2 Date of publication or
   most recent update
   ("n.d." if there is no
   date)
3 Title of section
4 Title of document
5 URL of section

WEB DOCUMENT CONTENTS PAGE

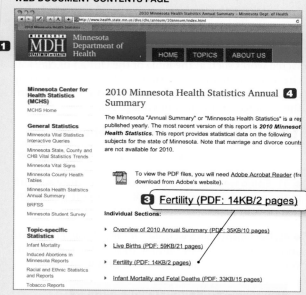

ON-SCREEN VIEW OF DOCUMENT

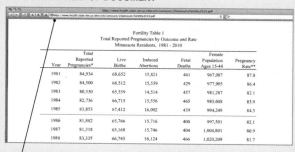

For more on citing documents from websites in APA style, see
items 42 and 43.

● **42. Document from a website (*cont.*)**

Wagner, D. A., Murphy, K. M., & De Korne, H. (2012, December).
*Learning first: A research agenda for improving learning
in low-income countries*. Retrieved from Brookings
Institution website: http://www.brookings.edu/research
/papers/2012/12/learning-first-wagner-murphy-de-korne

Centers for Disease Control and Prevention. (2012, December
10). *Concussion in winter sports*. Retrieved from http://
www.cdc.gov/Features/HockeyConcussions/index.html

● **43. Section in a web document**   Cite as a chapter in
a book or a selection in an anthology (see item 29b).

Chang, W.-Y., & Milan, L. M. (2012, October). Relationship
between degree field and emigration. In *International
mobility and employment characteristics among recent
recipients of U.S. doctorates*. Retrieved from National
Science Foundation website: http://www.nsf.gov
/statistics/infbrief/nsf13300

● **44. Blog post**   If the writer's real name and screen
name are given, put the real name first, followed by the
screen name in brackets.

Kerssen, T. (2012, October 5). Hunger is political: Food
Sovereignty Prize honors social movements [Blog post].
Retrieved from http://www.foodfirst.org/en/node/4020

● **45. Blog comment**

Studebakerhawk_14611. (2012, December 5). Re: A people's
history of MOOCs [Blog comment]. Retrieved from
http://www.insidehighered.com/blogs/library-babel-fish
/people's-history-moocs

14e Audio, visual, and multimedia sources

● **46. Podcast**

Schulz, K. (2011, March). *Kathryn Schulz: On being wrong* [Video
podcast]. Retrieved from TED on http://itunes.apple.com/

Taylor, A., & Parfitt, G. (2011, January 13). *Physical activity
and mental health: What's the evidence?* [Audio podcast].
Retrieved from Open University on http://itunes.apple.com/

● **47. Video or audio on the web**

Kurzen, B. (2012, April 5). *Going beyond Muslim-Christian
conflict in Nigeria* [Video file]. Retrieved from http://www
.youtube.com/watch?v=JD8MIJOA050

Bever, T., Piattelli-Palmarini, M., Hammond, M., Barss, A., &
Bergesen, A. (2012, February 2). *A basic introduction
to Chomsky's linguistics* [Audio file]. Retrieved from
University of Arizona, College of Social & Behavioral
Sciences, Department of Linguistics website: http://
linguistics.arizona.edu/node/711

● **48. Transcript of an audio or a video file**

Malone, T. W. (2012, November 21). *Collective intelligence*
[Transcript of video file]. Retrieved from http://edge.org
/conversation/collective-intelligence

● **49. Film (DVD, BD, or other format)**   In brackets following the title, add a description of the medium: "Motion
picture," "Video file," "DVD," "BD," and so on. For a
motion picture or a DVD or BD, add the location where
the film was made and the studio. If you retrieved the
film from the web or used a streaming service, give the
URL for the home page.

Affleck, B. (Director). (2012). *Argo* [Motion picture]. Burbank,
CA: Warner Bros.

Ross, G. (Director and Writer), & Collins, S. (Writer). (2012). *The hunger games* [Video file]. Retrieved from http://netflix.com/

● **50. Television or radio program**

a. Series

Hager, M. (Executive producer), & Schieffer, B. (Moderator). (2012). *Face the nation* [Television series]. Washington, DC: CBS News.

b. Episode on the web

Morton, D. (Producer). (2012). Fast times at West Philly High [Television series episode]. In M. Hager (Executive producer), *Frontline*. Retrieved from http://www.wgbh.org/

● **51. Music recording**

Chibalonza, A. Jubilee. (2012). On *African voices* [CD]. Merenberg, Germany: ZYX Music.

African voices [CD]. (2012). Merenberg, Germany: ZYX Music.

● **52. Lecture, speech, or address**

Verghese, A. (2012, December 6). *Colonialism and patterns of ethnic conflict in contemporary India*. Address at the Freeman Spogli Institute, Stanford University, Stanford, CA.

● **53. Data set or graphic representation of data (graph, chart, table)** If the item is numbered in the source, indicate the number in parentheses after the title. If the graphic appears within a larger document, do not italicize the title of the graphic.

U.S. Department of Agriculture, Economic Research Service. (2011). *Daily intake of nutrients by food source: 2005-08* [Data set]. Retrieved from http://www.ers.usda.gov/data -products/food-consumption-and-nutrient-intakes.aspx

Gallup. (2012, December 5). *In U.S., more cite obesity as most urgent health problem* [Graphs]. Retrieved from http:// www.gallup.com/poll/159083/cite-obesity-urgent-health -problem.aspx

● **54. Mobile application software (app)** Begin with the developer of the app, if known (as in the second example on p. 136).

MindNode Touch 2.3 [Mobile application software]. (2012).
    Retrieved from http://itunes.apple.com/

Source Tree Solutions. (2012). mojoPortal [Mobile application
    software]. Retrieved from http://www.microsoft.com/web
    /gallery/

● **55. Video game** If the game can be played on the
web or was downloaded from the web, give the URL
instead of publication information.

Firaxis Games. (2010). Sid Meier's civilization V [Video game].
    New York, NY: Take-Two Interactive. Xbox 360.

Atom Entertainment. (2012). Edgeworld [Video game].
    Retrieved from http://www.addictinggames.com/

● **56. Map**

Ukraine [Map]. (2008). Retrieved from the University of
    Texas at Austin Perry-Castañeda Library Map Collection
    website: http://www.lib.utexas.edu/maps/cia08/ukraine_
    sm_2008.gif

Syrian uprising map [Map]. (2012, October). Retrieved from
    http://www.polgeonow.com/2012/10/syria-uprising-map
    -october-2012-7.html

● **57. Advertisement**

VMware [Advertisement]. (2012, September). *Harvard Business
    Review, 90*(9), 27.

● **58. Work of art or photograph**

Olson, A. (2011). *Short story* [Painting]. Museum of
    Contemporary Art, Chicago, IL.

Crowner, S. (2012). *Kurtyna fragments* [Painting]. Retrieved
    from http://www.walkerart.org/

Weber, J. (1992). *Toward freedom* [Outdoor mural]. Sherman
    Oaks, CA.

● **59. Brochure or fact sheet**

National Council of State Boards of Nursing. (2011). *A nurse's
    guide to professional boundaries* [Brochure]. Retrieved
    from https://www.ncsbn.org/

World Health Organization. (2012, September). *Road traffic injuries* (No. 358) [Fact sheet]. Retrieved from http://www.who.int/mediacentre/factsheets/fs358/en/index.html

● **60. Press release**

Urban Institute. (2012, October 11). Two studies address health policy on campaign trail [Press release]. Retrieved from http://www.urban.org/publications/901537.html

● **61. Presentation slides**

Boeninger, C. F. (2008, August). *Web 2.0 tools for reference and instructional services* [Presentation slides]. Retrieved from http://libraryvoice.com/archives/2008/08/04/opal-20-conference-presentation-slides

● **62. Lecture notes or other course materials** Cite materials that your instructor has posted on the web as you would a web document or a section in a web document (see item 42 or 43). Cite other material from your instructor as personal communication in the text of your paper (see items 15 and 16 on p. 112).

Blum, R. (2011). Neurodevelopment in the first decade of life [Lecture notes and audio file]. In R. Blum & L. M. Blum, *Child health and development*. Retrieved from http://ocw.jhsph.edu/index.cfm/go/viewCourse/course/childhealth/coursePage/lectureNotes/

14f Personal communication and social media

● **63. Email** Email messages, letters, and other personal communication are not included in the list of references. (See item 15 on p. 112 for citing these sources in the text of your paper.)

● **64. Online posting** If an online posting is not archived, cite it as a personal communication in the text of your paper and do not include it in the list of references. If the posting is archived, give the URL and the name of the discussion list if it is not part of the URL.

McKinney, J. (2006, December 19). Adult education-healthcare partnerships [Electronic mailing list message]. Retrieved from http://www.nifl.gov/pipermail/healthliteracy/2006/000524.html

● **65. Social media** If the writer's real name and screen name are given, put the real name first, followed by the screen name in brackets. If only the screen name is known, begin with that name, not in brackets. Add the date of posting in parentheses (use "n.d." if the post has no date). For the title, include the entire post or a caption (up to 40 words); use a description of the post if there is no title or caption. After the title, add an appropriate label in brackets such as "Tweet," "Facebook status update," or "Photograph." Include the URL for the post. Provide a retrieval date only if the content is undated. Cite personal media posts that are not accessible to all readers as personal communication in the text of your paper (see item 15 on p. 112).

National Science Foundation. (2015, December 8). Simulation shows key to building powerful magnetic fields 1.usa.gov/1TZUiJ6 #supernovas #supercomputers [Tweet]. Retrieved from https://twitter.com/NSF /status/674352440582545413/

U.S. Department of Education. (2015, December 10). We're watching President Obama sign the Every Student Succeeds Act [Facebook post]. Retrieved from http://www.facebook .com/ED.gov/

15 APA notes

15a Footnotes in the text

Occasionally, you may use footnotes to provide additional material that is important but that might interrupt the flow of the paper. Notes should be brief and focused. Use notes sparingly; if the material will take more than a few sentences, you should consider integrating the information in the text or placing it in an appendix (see 10j).

In the text of your paper, use a superscript arabic numeral to indicate a note. At the bottom of the page, place the same superscript numeral and the text of the note. Number the notes consecutively throughout the paper. (See also "Footnotes" in 11a for more details.)

TEXT

Writer Charles Fishman (2007) noted in his article "The Wal-Mart You Don't Know"[1] that the retailer "does more business than Target, Sears, Kmart, J.C. Penney, Safeway, and Kroger combined."

FOOTNOTE

[1]In 2008, Wal-Mart changed the name of its stores to Walmart.

15b Notes in tables and figures

Notes in tables   A note at the bottom of a table can provide an explanation of terms used in the table, such as abbreviations and symbols. If your table contains data from an outside source or if you have taken or adapted the table from a source, give the source information directly following any explanation of terms.

If you need to explain specific information within the table, use lettered footnotes within the table and corresponding letters in the footnotes following the source information. (See also "Visuals" in 11a.)

TABLE NOTE

Note. Adapted from "The Flipped Class Demystified," n.d., retrieved from New York University website: https://www.nyu.edu/faculty /teaching-and-learning-resources/instructional-technology-support /instructional-design-assessment/flipped-classes/the-flipped-class -demystified.html.

Notes in figures   Each figure should have a number and a caption, a brief explanation of the content of the figure, at the bottom of the figure. If you have taken or adapted the figure from an outside source, give the source information immediately following the caption. (See also "Visuals" in 11a.)

FIGURE NOTE

Figure 1. This graph shows that many Americans consume about three times more fats and sugars and twice as many refined grains as is recommended but only half of the recommended foods. From United States, Department of Agriculture and Department of Health and Human Services, 2010, Figure 5-1.

Clarity

16   Tighten wordy sentences.

Long sentences are not necessarily wordy, nor are short
sentences always concise. A sentence is wordy if it can
be tightened without loss of meaning.

16a Redundancies

Redundancies such as *cooperate together*, *yellow in color*,
and *basic essentials* are a common source of wordiness.
There is no need to say the same thing twice.

▶   Daniel ~~is employed~~ at a private rehabilitation
     works

     center ~~working~~ as a physical therapist.

Modifiers are redundant when their meanings are suggested by other words in the sentence.

▶   Sylvia ~~very hurriedly~~ scribbled her name and

     phone number on the back of a greasy napkin.

16b Empty or inflated phrases

An empty word or phrase can be cut with little or no
loss of meaning. An inflated phrase can be reduced to
a word or two.

▶   ~~In my opinion,~~ *T*heir current immigration policy is

     misguided.

▶   Funds are limited ~~at this point in time.~~
                   now.

INFLATED	CONCISE
along the lines of	like
at the present time	now, currently
because of the fact that	because
by means of	by
due to the fact that	because
for the reason that	because
in order to	to
in spite of the fact that	although, though
in the event that	if
until such time as	until

16c Needlessly complex structures

Simplifying sentences and using stronger verbs can help make writing clearer and more direct.

▶ Researchers ~~were involved in examining~~ examined the effect of classical music on unborn babies.

▶ ~~It is imperative that~~ All night managers must follow strict procedures when locking the safe.

▶ The financial analyst claimed that because of volatile market conditions she could not ~~make an~~ estimate ~~of~~ the company's future profits.

17 Prefer active verbs.

As a rule, active verbs express meaning more vigorously than forms of the verb *be* or verbs in the passive voice. Forms of *be* (*be, am, is, are, was, were, being, been*) lack vigor because they convey no action. Passive verbs lack strength because their subjects receive the action instead of doing it.

Forms of *be* and passive verbs have legitimate uses, but choose an active verb whenever possible.

BE VERB   A surge of power *was* responsible for the destruction of the pumps.

PASSIVE   The pumps *were destroyed* by a surge of power.

ACTIVE   A surge of power *destroyed* the pumps.

17a When to replace *be* verbs

Not every *be* verb needs replacing. The forms of *be* (*be, am, is, are, was, were, being, been*) work well when you want to link a subject to a noun that clearly renames it or to an adjective that describes it: *Orchard House was the home of Louisa May Alcott. The harvest will be bountiful after the summer rains.*

If using a *be* verb makes a sentence needlessly wordy, consider replacing it. Often a phrase following the verb contains a noun or an adjective (such as *violation* or *resistant*) that suggests a more vigorous, active verb (*violate, resisted*).

▶ Burying nuclear waste in Antarctica would ~~be in~~
  ^violate^
  ~~violation of~~ an international treaty.

▶ When Rosa Parks ~~was resistant to~~ giving up her
  ^resisted^
  seat on the bus, she became a civil rights hero.

NOTE: When used as helping verbs with present participles to express ongoing action, *be* verbs are fine: *She was swimming when the whistle blew*. (See 26b.)

17b When to replace passive verbs

In the active voice, the subject of the sentence performs the action; in the passive, the subject receives the action.

ACTIVE   The committee *reached* a decision.

PASSIVE   A decision *was reached* by the committee.

In passive sentences, the actor (in this case *committee*) frequently does not appear: *A decision was reached.*

  In most cases, you will want to emphasize the actor, so you should use the active voice. To replace a passive verb with an active one, make the actor the subject of the sentence.

▶ ~~Samples were~~ collected daily from the stagnant
  ^Investigators^   ^samples^
  pond.

▶ ~~The land was stripped of timber before the settlers~~
  The settlers stripped the land of timber before realizing
  ~~realized~~ the consequences of their actions.

  The passive voice is appropriate when you wish to emphasize the receiver of the action or to minimize the importance of the actor. In the following sentence, for example, the writer intended to focus on the tobacco plants, not on the people spraying them: *As the time for harvest approaches, the tobacco plants are sprayed with a chemical to retard the growth of suckers*. (See also 2b.)

18   Balance parallel ideas.

If two or more ideas are parallel, they should be expressed in parallel grammatical form.

A kiss can be a comma, a question mark, or an exclamation point.
                                              —Mistinguett

This novel is not to be tossed lightly aside, but to be hurled with great force.
                                              —Dorothy Parker

18a   Items in a series

Balance all items in a series by presenting them in parallel grammatical form.

▶   Cross-training involves a variety of exercises, such
    as running, swimming, and ~~weights~~ lifting.

▶   Children who study music also learn confidence,
    discipline, and ~~they are creative~~ creativity.

▶   Racing to work, Sam drove down the middle of
    the road, ran one red light, and ignored two stop signs.

18b   Paired ideas

When pairing ideas, underscore their connection by expressing them in similar grammatical form. Paired ideas are usually connected in one of three ways: (1) with a coordinating conjunction such as *and*, *but*, or *or*; (2) with a correlative conjunction such as *either...or*, *neither...nor*, *not only...but also*, or *whether...or*; or (3) with a word introducing a comparison, usually *than* or *as*.

▶   Many states are reducing property taxes for home
    owners and ~~extend~~ extending financial aid in the form of tax
    credits to renters.

    The coordinating conjunction *and* connects two *-ing* verb
    forms: *reducing...extending*.

▶ **Thomas Edison was not only a prolific inventor**

but also ~~was~~ a successful entrepreneur.

The correlative conjunction *not only . . . but also* connects
two noun phrases: *a prolific inventor* and *a successful
entrepreneur.*

                                                 to ground
▶ **It is easier to speak in abstractions than ~~grounding~~**
                                                ^

one's thoughts in reality.

The comparative term *than* links two infinitive phrases:
to speak . . . to ground.

NOTE: Repeat function words such as prepositions (*by,
to*) and subordinating conjunctions (*that, because*) to
make parallel ideas easier to grasp.

▶ **Our study revealed that left-handed students were**

more likely to have trouble with classroom desks
    that
and rearranging desks for exam periods was
  ^
useful.

19   Add needed words.

Sometimes writers leave out words intentionally, without affecting meaning. But the result is often a confusing or an ungrammatical sentence. Readers need to see
at a glance how the parts of a sentence are connected.

19a Words in compound structures

In compound structures, words are often omitted for
economy: *Tom is a man who means what he says and
[who] says what he means.* Such omissions are acceptable as long as the omitted words are common to both
parts of the compound structure.

    If a sentence is ungrammatical because an omitted
word is not common to both parts of the compound
structure, the word must be put back in.

▶ Advertisers target customers whom they identify
  who
  through demographic research or have purchased

  their product in the past.

  The word *who* must be included because *whom . . . have
  purchased* is not grammatically correct.

  accepted
▶ Mayor Davidson never has and never will accept a

  bribe.

  Has . . . accept is not grammatically correct.

  in
▶ Many South Pacific tribes still believe and live by

  ancient laws.

  Believe . . . by is not idiomatic English.

19b The word *that*

Add the word *that* if there is any danger of misreading
without it.

▶ In his obedience experiments, psychologist
  that
  Stanley Milgram discovered ordinary people were

  willing to inflict physical pain on strangers.

  Milgram didn't discover people; he discovered that people were willing to inflict pain on strangers.

19c Words in comparisons

Comparisons should be between items that are alike.
To compare unlike items is illogical and distracting.

▶ The forests of North America are much more
  those of
  extensive than Europe.

  Comparisons should be complete so that readers
  will understand what is being compared.

INCOMPLETE Brand X is less salty.

COMPLETE Brand X is less salty than Brand Y.

Also, comparisons should leave no ambiguity about meaning. In the following sentence, two interpretations are possible.

AMBIGUOUS   Kai helped me more than my friend.

CLEAR   Kai helped me more than *he helped* my friend.

CLEAR   Kai helped me more than my friend *did*.

20   Eliminate confusing shifts.

20a   Shifts in point of view

The point of view of a piece of writing is the perspective from which it is written: first person (*I* or *we*), second person (*you*), or third person (*he, she, it, one,* or *they*). The *I* (or *we*) point of view, which emphasizes the writer, is a good choice for writing based primarily on personal experience. The *you* point of view, which emphasizes the reader, works well for giving advice or explaining how to do something. The third-person point of view, which emphasizes the subject, is appropriate in most academic and professional writing.

Writers who have trouble settling on an appropriate point of view sometimes shift confusingly from one to another. The solution is to choose a suitable perspective and then stay with it. (See also 27a.)

▶   Our class practiced rescuing a victim trapped in a
                   We   *our*
   wrecked car. ~~You~~ were graded on ~~your~~ speed and

   skill in freeing the victim.

    You
▶   ~~Travelers~~ need a signed passport for trips abroad.

   You should also fill out the emergency information

   page in the passport.

20b   Shifts in tense

Consistent verb tenses clearly establish the time of the actions being described. When a passage begins in one tense and then shifts without warning and for no reason to another, readers are distracted and confused.

▶ **There was no way I could fight the current and**
                                                      jumped
win. Just as I was losing hope, a stranger ~~jumps~~
                                     swam
off a passing boat and ~~swims~~ toward me.
                           ^

Writers often shift verb tenses when writing about
literature. The literary convention is to describe fictional
events consistently in the present tense. (See 26b.)

21 Untangle mixed constructions.

A mixed construction contains sentence parts that do
not sensibly fit together. The mismatch may be a matter of grammar or of logic.

21a Mixed grammar

You should not begin a sentence with one grammatical plan and then switch without warning to another.
Rethinking the purpose of the sentence can help you
revise.
        M
▶ **~~For~~ most drivers who have a blood alcohol level of**
       ^
   .05 percent increase their risk of causing an accident.

The prepositional phrase beginning with *For* cannot
serve as the subject of the verb *increase*. The revision
makes *drivers* the subject.

▶ **Although the United States is a wealthy nation, ~~but~~**
   more than 20 percent of our children live in poverty.

The coordinating conjunction *but* cannot link a subordinate clause (*Although...*) with an independent clause
(*more than 20 percent...*).

21b Illogical connections

A sentence's subject and verb should make sense together.

                     the double personal exemption for
▶ **Under the revised plan, the elderly/~~who now receive~~**
                                   ^
   ~~a double personal exemption,~~ will be abolished.

The exemption, not the elderly, will be abolished.

Tiffany
▶ The court decided that ~~Tiffany's welfare~~ would not

be safe living with her abusive parents.

Tiffany, not her welfare, would not be safe.

21c *Is when*, *is where*, and *reason...is because* constructions

In formal English, readers sometimes object to *is when*, *is where*, and *reason...is because* constructions on grammatical or logical grounds.

a disorder suffered by people who
▶ Anorexia nervosa is ~~where people~~ think they are

too fat and diet to the point of starvation.

Anorexia nervosa is a disorder, not a place.

T
▶ ~~The reason~~ the experiment failed ~~is~~ because

conditions in the lab were not sterile.

22 Repair misplaced and dangling modifiers.

Modifiers should point clearly to the words they modify. As a rule, related words should be kept together.

22a Misplaced words

Limiting modifiers such as *only*, *even*, *almost*, *nearly*, and *just* should appear in front of a verb only if they modify the verb. If they limit the meaning of some other word in the sentence, they should be placed in front of that word.

only
▶ Medical lasers ~~only~~ destroy the target, leaving the

surrounding healthy tissue intact.

even
▶ I couldn't ~~even~~ save a dollar out of my paycheck.

When the limiting modifier *not* is misplaced, the sentence usually suggests a meaning the writer did not intend.

▶ In the United States in 1860, all black southerners ^not^ were ~~not~~ slaves.

The original sentence means that no black southerners were slaves. The revision makes the writer's real meaning clear.

22b Misplaced phrases and clauses

Although phrases and clauses can appear at some distance from the words they modify, make sure your meaning is clear. When phrases or clauses are oddly placed, absurd misreadings can result.

▶ ~~There~~ are many pictures of comedians who have ^On the walls^

performed at Gavin's. ~~on the walls.~~

The comedians weren't performing on the walls; the pictures were on the walls.

▶ The robber was described as a 6-foot-tall man ^170-pound,^

with a mustache. ~~weighing 170 pounds.~~

The robber, not the mustache, weighed 170 pounds.

22c Dangling modifiers

A dangling modifier fails to refer logically to any word in the sentence. Dangling modifiers are usually introductory word groups (such as verbal phrases) that suggest but do not name an actor. When a sentence opens with such a modifier, readers expect the subject of the next clause to name the actor. If it doesn't, the modifier dangles.

DANGLING   Upon entering the doctor's office, a skeleton caught my attention.

This sentence suggests—absurdly—that the skeleton entered the doctor's office.

To repair a dangling modifier, you can revise the sentence in one of two ways:

1. Name the actor in the subject of the sentence.
2. Name the actor in the modifier.

> I noticed
> Upon entering the doctor's office, a skeleton.
>   ^   ^
>
> ~~caught my attention.~~

> As I entered
> ~~Upon entering~~ the doctor's office, a skeleton
>   ^
>
> caught my attention.

You cannot repair a dangling modifier simply by moving it: *A skeleton caught my attention upon entering the doctor's office.* The sentence still suggests that the skeleton entered the doctor's office.

> Wanting to create checks and balances on power,
>   the framers of
>   the Constitution divided the government into
>   ^
>
>   three branches.

The framers (not the Constitution itself) wanted to create checks and balances.

>   women were often denied
> After completing seminary training, ~~women's~~
>   ^
>
>   access to the priesthood. ~~was often denied.~~
>   ^

The women (not their access to the priesthood) completed the training. The writer has revised the sentence by making *women* (not *women's access*) the subject.

22d Split infinitives

An infinitive consists of *to* plus a verb: *to think, to dance.* When a modifier appears between its two parts, an infinitive is said to be "split": *to slowly drive.* If a split infinitive is awkward, move the modifier to another position in the sentence.

> Cardiologists encourage their patients to
>   more carefully.
>   ~~more carefully~~ watch their cholesterol levels/
>   ^

Attempts to avoid split infinitives sometimes result in awkward sentences. When alternative phrasing sounds unnatural, most experts allow—and even encourage—splitting the infinitive. *We decided to actually enforce the law* is a natural construction in English. *We decided actually to enforce the law* is not.

23 Provide sentence variety.

Sentence variety can help keep readers interested in your writing. If most of your sentences are the same length or begin the same way, try combining them or varying sentence starters.

23a Combining choppy sentences

If a series of short sentences sounds choppy, consider combining sentences. Look for opportunities to tuck some of your ideas into subordinate clauses. A subordinate clause, which contains a subject and a verb, begins with a word such as *after, although, because, before, if, since, that, unless, until, when, where, which,* or *who.* (See 29a.)

▶ We keep our use of insecticides to a minimum/
  because we
  ~~We~~ are concerned about the environment.
     ^

Also look for opportunities to tuck some of your ideas into phrases, word groups that lack a subject and a verb. You will usually see more than one way to combine choppy sentences; the method you choose should depend on the details you want to emphasize.

▶ The Chesapeake and Ohio Canal, ~~is~~ a 184-mile water-
                                  ^
  way constructed in the 1800s/. ~~It~~ was a major source
                                 ^
  of transportation for goods during the Civil War.

This revision emphasizes the significance of the canal during the Civil War. The first sentence, about the age of the canal, has been made into a phrase modifying *Chesapeake and Ohio Canal.*

   Used as a major source of transportation for goods
   during the Civil War, the
▶ ~~The~~ Chesapeake and Ohio Canal is a 184-mile water-
     ^
  way constructed in the 1800s. ~~It was a major source~~

  ~~of transportation for goods during the Civil War.~~

This revision emphasizes the age of the canal. The second sentence, about the canal's use for transportation of goods, has become a participial phrase modifying *Chesapeake and Ohio Canal.* (See 23b.)

When short sentences contain ideas of equal importance, it is often effective to combine them with *and*,
but, or *or*.

▶   Shore houses were flooded up to the first floor/, ^and^

    Brant's Lighthouse was swallowed by the sea.

23b Varying sentence openings

Most sentences in English begin with the subject, move
to the verb, and continue to an object, with modifiers
tucked in along the way or put at the end. For the most
part, such sentences are fine. Put too many of them in
a row, however, and they become monotonous.

Words, phrases, or clauses modifying the verb can
often be inserted ahead of the subject.

▶   ^Eventually a^ A̶ few drops of sap ~~eventually~~ began to trickle into
    the pail.

▶   ^Just as the sun was coming up, a^ A̶ pair of black ducks flew over the pond. ~~just as~~
    ~~the sun was coming up.~~

Participial phrases (beginning with verb forms such
as *driving* or *exhausted*) can frequently be moved to the
start of a sentence without loss of clarity.

▶   ~~The committee,~~ ^D^discouraged by the researchers'
    apparent lack of progress, ^the committee^ nearly withdrew
    funding for the prizewinning experiments.

NOTE: In a sentence that begins with a participial phrase,
the subject of the sentence must name the person or
thing being described. If it doesn't, the phrase dangles.
(See 22c.)

24   Find an appropriate voice.

An appropriate voice is one that suits your subject,
engages your audience, and conforms to the conventions of the genre in which you are writing, such as

analytical essays, lab reports, research papers, business memos, and so on.

In academic and professional writing, certain language is generally considered inappropriate: jargon, clichés, slang, and sexist or biased language.

24a Jargon

Jargon is specialized language used among members of a trade, profession, or group. Use jargon only when readers will be familiar with it or when plain English will not do as well.

JARGON   We outsourced the work to an outfit in Ohio because we didn't have the bandwidth to tackle it in-house.

REVISED We hired a company in Ohio because we had too few employees to do the work.

Broadly defined, jargon includes puffed-up language designed more to impress readers than to inform them. The following are common examples from business, government, higher education, and the military, with plain English translations in parentheses.

commence (begin)	indicator (sign)
components (parts)	optimal (best)
endeavor (try)	parameters (boundaries, limits)
facilitate (help)	prior to (before)
finalize (finish)	utilize (use)
impact (v.) (affect)	viable (workable)

Sentences filled with jargon are hard to read and often wordy.

▶ The CEO should ~~dialogue~~ talk with investors about ~~partnering~~ working with clients to buy land in ~~economically deprived zones.~~ poor neighborhoods.

▶ All ~~employees functioning in the capacity of~~ work-study students ~~are required to give evidence of current enrollment.~~ must prove that they are currently enrolled.

24b Clichés

The pioneer who first announced that he had "slept like a log" no doubt amused his companions with a fresh and unlikely comparison. Today, however, that comparison is a cliché, a saying that can no longer add emphasis or surprise. To see just how predictable clichés are, put your hand over the right-hand column below and then finish the phrases given on the left.

beat around the	bush
busy as a	bee, beaver
cool as a	cucumber
crystal	clear
light as a	feather
like a bull	in a china shop
playing with	fire
selling like	hotcakes
water under the	bridge
white as a	sheet, ghost
avoid clichés like the	plague

The solution for clichés is simple: Just delete them. Sometimes you can write around a cliché by adding an element of surprise. One student who had written that she had butterflies in her stomach revised her cliché like this:

> If all of the action in my stomach is caused by butterflies, there must be a horde of them, with horseshoes on.

The image of butterflies wearing horseshoes is fresh and unlikely, not predictable like the original cliché.

24c Slang

Slang is an informal and sometimes private vocabulary that expresses the solidarity of a group such as teenagers, rap musicians, or sports fans. Although it does have a certain vitality, slang is a code that not everyone understands, and it is too informal for most written work.

> ▶ When the server crashed, 3 hours of unsaved *we lost* data. ~~went down the tubes.~~

24d Sexist language

Sexist language excludes, stereotypes, or demeans women or men and should be avoided. Using nonsexist language shows respect for and sensitivity to your readers.

In your writing, avoid referring to any one profession as exclusively male or exclusively female (teachers as women or engineers as men, for example). Also avoid using different conventions when identifying women and men.

▶ All executives' ~~wives~~ *spouses* are invited to the picnic.

▶ Boris Stotsky, attorney, and ~~Mrs.~~ Cynthia Jones, ~~mother of three,~~ *graphic designer,* are running for city council.

Traditionally, *he*, *him*, and *his* were used to refer generically to persons of either sex: *A journalist is motivated by his deadline.* When revising such sexist language, you may be tempted to substitute *he or she* and *his or her*. This strategy is wordy and awkward when repeated throughout an essay. Also, the phrases *he or she* and *his or her* exclude people who do not identify as *he* or *she*. A better strategy is to write in the plural or to revise the sentence to avoid the problem.

▶ ~~A journalist is~~ *Journalists are* motivated by ~~his deadline.~~ *their deadlines.*

▶ A journalist is motivated by ~~his~~ *a* deadline.

Like *he* and *his*, the nouns *man* and *men* and related words were once used generically to refer to persons of either sex. Use gender-neutral terms instead.

INAPPROPRIATE	APPROPRIATE
chairman	chairperson, chair
congressman	representative, legislator
fireman	firefighter
mailman	mail carrier, postal worker
mankind	people, humans
to man (v.)	to operate, to staff
weatherman	meteorologist, forecaster

Grammar

25 Make subjects and verbs agree.

In the present tense, verbs agree with their subjects in number (singular or plural) and in person (first, second, or third). The present-tense ending -s is used on a verb if its subject is third-person singular; otherwise the verb takes no ending. Consider, for example, the present-tense forms of the verb *give.*

	SINGULAR	**PLURAL**
FIRST PERSON	I give	we give
SECOND PERSON	you give	you give
THIRD PERSON	he/she/it gives	they give
	Yolanda gives	parents give

The verb *be* varies from this pattern; it has special forms in *both* the present and the past tense.

PRESENT-TENSE FORMS OF *BE*		**PAST-TENSE FORMS OF *BE***	
I am	we are	I was	we were
you are	you are	you were	you were
he/she/it is	they are	he/she/it was	they were

This section describes particular situations that can cause problems with subject-verb agreement.

25a Words between subject and verb

Word groups often come between the subject and the verb. Such word groups, usually modifying the subject, may contain a noun that at first appears to be the subject. By mentally stripping away such modifiers, you can isolate the noun that is in fact the subject.

The *samples* on the tray in the lab *need* testing.

▶ High levels of air pollution damages the

respiratory tract.

The subject is *levels*, not *pollution*.

has
▶ The slaughter of pandas for their pelts ~~have~~ caused
         ^
the panda population to decline drastically.

The subject is *slaughter*, not *pandas* or *pelts*.

NOTE: Phrases beginning with the prepositions *as well as*, *in addition to*, *accompanied by*, *together with*, and *along with* do not make a singular subject plural: *The governor as well as his press secretary was* [not *were*] *on the plane.*

25b Subjects joined with *and*

Compound subjects joined with *and* are nearly always plural.

▶ Bleach and ammonia creates a toxic gas when mixed.

EXCEPTION: If the parts of the subject form a single unit, you may treat the subject as singular: *Bacon and eggs is always on the menu.*

25c Subjects joined with *or* or *nor*

With compound subjects joined with *or* or *nor,* make the verb agree with the part of the subject nearer to the verb.

▶ If an infant or a child ~~have~~ a high fever, call a doctor.
    has

▶ Neither the lab assistant nor the students ~~was~~ able
    were

    to download the program.

25d Indefinite pronouns such as *someone*

Indefinite pronouns refer to nonspecific persons or things. The following indefinite pronouns are singular: *anybody, anyone, anything, each, either, everybody, everyone, everything, neither, nobody, no one, somebody, someone, something.*

▶ Nobody who participated in the taste tests ~~were~~ paid.
    was

▶ Each of the essays ~~have~~ been graded.
    has

A few indefinite pronouns (*all, any, none, some*) may be singular or plural depending on the noun or pronoun they refer to: *Some of our luggage was lost. Some of the rocks were slippery. None of his advice makes sense. None of the eggs were broken.*

25e Collective nouns such as *jury*

Collective nouns such as *jury, committee, audience, crowd, class, family*, and *couple* name a group. In American English, collective nouns are usually treated as singular: They emphasize the group as a unit.

▶ The board of trustees ~~meet~~ in Denver twice a year.
   ^meets^

   Occasionally, to draw attention to the individual members of the group, a collective noun may be treated as plural: *The class is debating among themselves.* Many writers prefer to add a clearly plural noun such as *members*: *The class members are debating among themselves.*

NOTE: In general, when fractions or units of measurement are used with a singular noun, treat them as singular; when they are used with a plural noun, treat them as plural: *Three-fourths of the pie has been eaten. One-fourth of the drivers were texting.*

25f Subject after verb

Verbs ordinarily follow subjects. When this normal order is reversed, it is easy to be confused.

▶ Of particular concern ~~is~~ penicillin and tetracycline,
   ^are^

   antibiotics used to make animals more resistant

   to disease.

   The subject, *penicillin and tetracycline*, is plural.

   The subject always follows the verb in sentences beginning with *there is* or *there are* (or *there was* or *there were*).

▶ There ~~was~~ a turtle and a snake in the tank.
   ^were^

   The subject, *turtle and snake*, is plural, so the verb must be *were*.

25g *Who, which,* and *that*

Like most pronouns, the relative pronouns *who, which,* and *that* have antecedents, nouns or pronouns to which they refer. Relative pronouns used as subjects of subordinate clauses take verbs that agree with their antecedents.

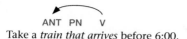

ANT PN　V
Take a *train that arrives* before 6:00.

Constructions such as *one of the students who* (or *one of the things that*) may cause problems for writers. Do not assume that the antecedent must be *one*. Instead, consider the logic of the sentence.

▶　**Our ability to use language is one of the things**
　　　　set
　　that ~~sets~~ us apart from animals.

The antecedent of *that* is *things*, not *one*. Several things set us apart from animals.

When the phrase *the only* comes before *one*, you are safe in assuming that *one* is the antecedent of the relative pronoun.

　　　　　　　　　　　　　　　　　　　　lives
▶　**Carmen is the only one of my friends who ~~live~~**

　　in my building.

The antecedent of *who* is *one*, not *friends*. Only one friend lives in the building.

25h Plural form, singular meaning

Words such as *athletics, economics, mathematics, physics, politics, statistics, measles,* and *news* are usually singular, despite their plural form.

　　　is
▶　**Politics ~~are~~ among my mother's favorite pastimes.**

EXCEPTION: Occasionally some of these words, especially *economics, mathematics, politics,* and *statistics,* have plural meanings: *Office politics often affect decisions about hiring and promotion. The economics of the building plan are prohibitive.*

25i Titles, company names, and words mentioned as words

Titles, company names, and words mentioned as words are singular.

▶ *Lost Cities* ~~describe~~ the discoveries of 50 ancient
  _{describes}

  civilizations.

▶ *Delmonico Brothers* ~~specialize~~ in organic produce
  _{specializes}

  and additive-free meats.

▶ *Controlled substances* ~~are~~ a euphemism for illegal
  _{is}

  drugs.

26 Be alert to other problems with verbs.

Section 25 deals with subject-verb agreement. This section describes a few other potential problems with verbs.

26a Irregular verbs

For all regular verbs, the past-tense and past-participle forms are the same, ending in *-ed* or *-d*, so there is no danger of confusion. This is not true, however, for irregular verbs, such as the following.

BASE FORM	PAST TENSE	PAST PARTICIPLE
break	broke	broken
fly	flew	flown
go	went	gone

The past-tense form, which never has a helping verb, expresses action that occurred entirely in the past. The past participle is used with a helping verb — either with *has, have,* or *had* to form one of the perfect tenses or with *be, am, is, are, was, were, being,* or *been* to form the passive voice.

PAST TENSE   Last July, we *went* to Beijing.

PAST PARTICIPLE We have *gone* to Beijing twice.

When you aren't sure which verb form to choose (*went* or *gone*, *broke* or *broken*, and so on), consult the list that begins at the bottom of the next page. Choose the past-tense form if your sentence doesn't have a helping verb; choose the past-participle form if it does.

▶ Yesterday we ~~seen~~ ^{saw} a film about rain forests.
  ^

Because there is no helping verb, the past-tense form *saw* is required.

▶ By the end of the day, the stock market had ~~fell~~ ^{fallen}
  ^
200 points.

Because of the helping verb *had*, the past-participle form *fallen* is required.

Distinguishing between *lie* and *lay* Writers often confuse the forms of *lie* (meaning "to recline or rest on a surface") and *lay* (meaning "to put or place something"). The intransitive verb *lie* does not take a direct object: *The tax forms lie on the table.* The transitive verb *lay* takes a direct object: *Please lay the tax forms on the table.*

In addition to confusing the meanings of *lie* and *lay*, writers are often unfamiliar with the Standard English forms of these verbs.

BASE FORM	PAST TENSE	PAST PARTICIPLE	PRESENT PARTICIPLE
lie	lay	lain	lying
lay	laid	laid	laying

Elizabeth was so exhausted that she *lay* down for a nap. [Past tense of *lie*, meaning "to recline"]

The prosecutor *laid* the photograph on a table close to the jurors. [Past tense of *lay*, meaning "to place"]

Letters dating from the Civil War were *lying* in the corner of the chest. [Present participle of *lie*]

The patient had *lain* in an uncomfortable position all night. [Past participle of *lie*]

Common irregular verbs

BASE FORM	PAST TENSE	PAST PARTICIPLE
arise	arose	arisen
awake	awoke, awaked	awaked, awoken
be	was, were	been
beat	beat	beaten, beat
become	became	become
begin	began	begun
bend	bent	bent

BASE FORM	PAST TENSE	PAST PARTICIPLE
bite	bit	bitten, bit
blow	blew	blown
break	broke	broken
bring	brought	brought
build	built	built
burst	burst	burst
buy	bought	bought
catch	caught	caught
choose	chose	chosen
cling	clung	clung
come	came	come
cost	cost	cost
deal	dealt	dealt
dig	dug	dug
dive	dived, dove	dived
do	did	done
draw	drew	drawn
dream	dreamed, dreamt	dreamed, dreamt
drink	drank	drunk
drive	drove	driven
eat	ate	eaten
fall	fell	fallen
fight	fought	fought
find	found	found
fly	flew	flown
forget	forgot	forgotten, forgot
freeze	froze	frozen
get	got	gotten, got
give	gave	given
go	went	gone
grow	grew	grown
hang (execute)	hanged	hanged
hang (suspend)	hung	hung
have	had	had
hear	heard	heard
hide	hid	hidden
hurt	hurt	hurt
keep	kept	kept
know	knew	known
lay (put)	laid	laid
lead	led	led

BASE FORM	PAST TENSE	PAST PARTICIPLE
lend	lent	lent
let (allow)	let	let
lie (recline)	lay	lain
lose	lost	lost
make	made	made
prove	proved	proved, proven
read	read	read
ride	rode	ridden
ring	rang	rung
rise (get up)	rose	risen
run	ran	run
say	said	said
see	saw	seen
send	sent	sent
set (place)	set	set
shake	shook	shaken
shoot	shot	shot
shrink	shrank	shrunk, shrunken
sing	sang	sung
sink	sank	sunk
sit (be seated)	sat	sat
slay	slew	slain
sleep	slept	slept
speak	spoke	spoken
spin	spun	spun
spring	sprang	sprung
stand	stood	stood
steal	stole	stolen
sting	stung	stung
strike	struck	struck, stricken
swear	swore	sworn
swim	swam	swum
swing	swung	swung
take	took	taken
teach	taught	taught
throw	threw	thrown
wake	woke, waked	waked, woken
wear	wore	worn
win	won	won
wring	wrung	wrung
write	wrote	written

26b Tense

Tenses indicate the time of an action in relation to the time of the speaking or writing about that action. The most common problem with tenses—shifting from one tense to another—is discussed in 20b. Other problems with tenses are detailed in this section, after the following survey of tenses.

Survey of tenses Tenses are classified as present, past, and future, with simple, perfect, and progressive forms for each.

The simple tenses indicate relatively simple time relations. The *simple present* tense is used primarily for actions occurring at the time they are being discussed or for actions occurring regularly. The *simple past* tense is used for actions completed in the past. The *simple future* tense is used for actions that will occur in the future. In the following table, the simple tenses are given for the regular verb *walk,* the irregular verb *ride,* and the highly irregular verb *be.*

SIMPLE PRESENT

SINGULAR		PLURAL	
I	walk, ride, am	we	walk, ride, are
you	walk, ride, are	you	walk, ride, are
he/she/it	walks, rides, is	they	walk, ride, are

SIMPLE PAST

SINGULAR		PLURAL	
I	walked, rode, was	we	walked, rode, were
you	walked, rode, were	you	walked, rode, were
he/she/it	walked, rode, was	they	walked, rode, were

SIMPLE FUTURE

I, you, he/she/it, we, they   will walk, ride, be

A verb in one of the perfect tenses (a form of *have* plus the past participle) expresses an action that was or will be completed at the time of another action.

PRESENT PERFECT

I, you, we, they	have walked, ridden, been
he/she/it	has walked, ridden, been

PAST PERFECT

I, you, he/she/it, we, they   had walked, ridden, been

FUTURE PERFECT

I, you, he/she/it, we, they   will have walked, ridden, been

Each of the six tenses has a progressive form used to describe actions in progress. A progressive verb consists of a form of *be* followed by the present participle.

PRESENT PROGRESSIVE

I	am walking, riding, being
he/she/it	is walking, riding, being
you, we, they	are walking, riding, being

PAST PROGRESSIVE

I, he/she/it	was walking, riding, being
you, we, they	were walking, riding, being

FUTURE PROGRESSIVE

I, you, he/she/it, we, they   will be walking, riding, being

PRESENT PERFECT PROGRESSIVE

I, you, we, they	have been walking, riding, being
he/she/it	has been walking, riding, being

PAST PERFECT PROGRESSIVE

I, you, he/she/it, we, they   had been walking, riding, being

FUTURE PERFECT PROGRESSIVE

I, you, he/she/it, we, they   will have been walking, riding, being

Special uses of the present tense   Use the present tense to refer to applications or effects of your own research results and to describe established knowledge.

► Our data indicated that concentrated poverty
   increases
   ~~increased~~ the likelihood of property crimes.
   ^

                              revolves
► Galileo taught that the earth ~~revolved~~ around the
                              ^
   sun.

See also 9b and the next section for uses of the past and present perfect tenses.

Note that in the humanities the present tense is used for writing about literary works.

is
▶ The scarlet letter ~~was~~ a punishment placed on
                    ^
                                          is
Hester's breast by the community, and yet it ~~was~~ an
                                                  ^
imaginative product of Hester's own needlework.

Special uses of the past and present perfect tenses
Especially in literature reviews and primary research papers, use the past tense or present perfect tense to discuss your own findings or the work of others. (See also 9b; see the previous section for uses of the present tense.)

                              explored
▶ In "On Violence," Arendt (1970) ~~explores~~ the
                                    ^
relationship between violence and power.

26c Mood

There are three moods in English: the *indicative*, used for facts, opinions, and questions; the *imperative*, used for orders or advice; and the *subjunctive*, used to express wishes, requests, or conditions contrary to fact. For many writers, the subjunctive is especially challenging.

For wishes and in *if* clauses expressing conditions contrary to fact, the subjunctive is the past-tense form of the verb; in the case of *be*, it is always *were* (not *was*), even if the subject is singular.

I wish that Jamal *drove* more slowly late at night.

If I *were* a member of Congress, I would vote for the bill.

TIP: Do not use the subjunctive mood in *if* clauses expressing conditions that exist or may exist: *If Danielle passes* [not *passed*] *the test, she will become a lifeguard.*

Use the subjunctive mood in *that* clauses following verbs such as *ask*, *insist*, *recommend*, and *request*. The subjunctive in such cases is the base form of the verb.

Dr. Chung insists that her students *be* on time.

We recommend that Dawson *file* form 1050 soon.

27 Use pronouns with care.

Pronouns are words that substitute for nouns: *he, it, them, her, me,* and so on. Pronoun errors are typically related to the four topics discussed in this section:

a. pronoun-antecedent agreement (singular vs. plural)
b. pronoun reference (clarity)
c. pronoun case (personal pronouns such as *I* vs. *me*)
d. pronoun case (*who* vs. *whom*)

27a Pronoun-antecedent agreement

The antecedent of a pronoun is the word the pronoun refers to. A pronoun and its antecedent agree when they are both singular or both plural.

SINGULAR   The *doctor* finished *her* rounds.

PLURAL   The *doctors* finished *their* rounds.

Indefinite pronouns   Indefinite pronouns refer to non-specific persons or things: *anybody, anyone, anything, each, either, everybody, everyone, everything, neither, nobody, no one, nothing, somebody, someone, something.* Traditionally, indefinite pronouns have been treated as singular in formal English. However, using a singular pronoun usually results in a sentence that is sexist, and the traditional alternative (*he* or *she*) excludes people who prefer not to refer to themselves as *he* or *she.* It is therefore becoming increasingly acceptable to use the plural pronoun *they* to refer to an indefinite pronoun.

SEXIST   *Everyone* performs at *his* own fitness level.

NONINCLUSIVE   *Everyone* performs at *his* or *her* own fitness level.

INCLUSIVE   *Everyone* performs at *their* own fitness level.

The following are typically your best options for revision:

1. Make the antecedent plural.
2. Rewrite the sentence to avoid the problem.

singers want   they

▶ If ~~someone wants~~ to audition, ~~he~~ should sign up.
  ^   ^

Someone who

▶ ~~If someone~~ wants to audition, ~~he~~ should sign up.
  ^

Generic nouns   A generic noun represents a typical member of a group, such as *a student*, or any member of a group, such as *any lawyer*. Although generic nouns may seem to have plural meanings, traditionally they have been considered to be singular.

Every *runner* must train rigorously if *he or she wants* [not *they want*] to excel.

For a plural pronoun that refers to a generic noun, you will usually have the same revision options as for indefinite pronouns.

Medical students

▶ ~~A medical student~~ must study hard if they want to
  ^

succeed.

▶ A medical student must study hard ~~if they want~~ to

succeed.

Collective nouns   Collective nouns such as *jury, committee, audience, crowd, family,* and *team* name a group. In American English, collective nouns are usually singular because they emphasize the group functioning as a unit.

The planning *committee* granted *its* [not *their*] permission to build.

If the members of the group function individually, however, you may treat the noun as plural: *The family put their signatures on the document.* Or you might add a plural antecedent such as *members* to the sentence: *The family members put their signatures on the document.*

27b Pronoun reference

In the sentence *When Andrew got home, he went straight to bed*, the noun *Andrew* is the antecedent of the pronoun *he*. A pronoun should refer clearly to its antecedent.

Ambiguous reference Ambiguous reference occurs when the pronoun could refer to two possible antecedents.

▶ *The cake collapsed when Aunt Harriet put it*
~~When Aunt Harriet put the cake~~ on the table~~/.~~ ~~it~~
^
~~collapsed.~~
^

▶ *"You have*
Tom told James, ~~that he had~~ won the lottery."
^   ^

What collapsed—the cake or the table? Who won the lottery—Tom or James? The revisions eliminate the ambiguity.

Implied reference A pronoun must refer to a specific antecedent, not to a word that is implied but not actually stated.

▶ *the braids*
After braiding Ann's hair, Sue decorated ~~them~~ with
^
ribbons.

Vague reference of *this*, *that*, or *which* The pronouns *this*, *that*, and *which* should ordinarily refer to specific antecedents rather than to whole ideas or sentences. When a pronoun's reference is too vague, either replace the pronoun with a noun or supply an antecedent to which the pronoun clearly refers.

▶ Television advertising has created new demands
the ads
for prescription drugs. People respond to ~~this~~ by
^
asking for drugs they may not need.

▶ Romeo and Juliet were both too young to have
a fact
acquired much wisdom, ~~and~~ that accounts for
^
their rash actions.

Indefinite reference of *they*, *it*, or *you* The pronoun *they* should refer to a specific antecedent. Do not use *they* to refer indefinitely to persons who have not been specifically mentioned.

▶ *The board*
~~They~~ announced an increase in sports fees for all
^
student athletes.

The word *it* should not be used indefinitely in constructions such as *In the article, it says that...*

▶   ~~In the~~ ^{The} encyclopedia/~~it~~ states that male moths can

smell female moths from several miles away.

The pronoun *you* is appropriate only when the writer is addressing the reader directly: *Once you have kneaded the dough, let it rise in a warm place.* Except in informal contexts, however, *you* should not be used to mean "anyone in general." Use a noun instead, as in the following example.

▶   **Ms. Pickersgill's *Guide to Etiquette* stipulates that**
a guest
~~you~~ **should not arrive at a party too early or leave**

too late.

27c Case of personal pronouns (*I* vs. *me* etc.)

The personal pronouns in the following chart change what is known as *case form* according to their grammatical function in a sentence. Pronouns functioning as subjects or subject complements appear in the *subjective* case; those functioning as objects appear in the *objective* case; and those showing ownership appear in the *possessive* case.

	SUBJECTIVE CASE	OBJECTIVE CASE	POSSESSIVE CASE
SINGULAR	I	me	my
	you	you	your
	he/she/it	him/her/it	his/her/its
PLURAL	we	us	our
	you	you	your
	they	them	their

Pronouns in the subjective and objective cases are frequently confused. Most of the rules in this section specify when to use one or the other of these cases (*I* or *me, he* or *him,* and so on).

Compound word groups   You may sometimes be confused when a subject or an object appears as part of a compound structure. To test for the correct pronoun,

mentally strip away all of the compound structure
except the pronoun in question.

▶ While diving for pearls, Ikiko and ~~her~~ ^she^ found a

sunken boat.

Ikiko and she is the subject of the verb *found.* Strip away
the words *Ikiko and* to test for the correct pronoun: *she
found* [not *her found*].

▶ The most traumatic experience for her father and
~~I~~ ^me^ occurred long after her operation.

Her father and me is the object of the preposition *for.*
Strip away the words *her father and* to test for the correct
pronoun: *for me* [not *for I*].

When in doubt about the correct pronoun, some
writers try to evade the choice by using a reflexive pronoun such as *myself.* Using a reflexive pronoun in such
situations is nonstandard.

▶ The cabdriver gave my husband and ~~myself~~ ^me^ some

good tips on traveling in New Delhi.

My husband and me is the indirect object of the verb
gave.

Appositives   Appositives are noun phrases that rename
nouns or pronouns. A pronoun used as an appositive
has the same function (usually subject or object) as the
word(s) it renames.

▶ The chief strategists, Dr. Bell and ~~me,~~ ^I,^ could not

agree on a plan.

The appositive *Dr. Bell and I* renames the subject,
strategists. Test: *I could not agree on a plan* [not *me could
not agree on a plan*].

▶ The reporter interviewed only two witnesses, the
shopkeeper and ~~I.~~ ^me.^

The appositive *the shopkeeper and me* renames the direct
object, *witnesses.* Test: *interviewed me* [not *interviewed I*].

Subject complements Use subjective-case pronouns for subject complements, which rename or describe the subject and usually follow *be, am, is, are, was, were, being,* or *been.*

▶   During the Lindbergh trial, Bruno Hauptmann
                                       he.
    repeatedly denied that the kidnapper was ~~him.~~
                                         ^

    If *kidnapper was he* seems too stilted, rewrite the sentence: *During the Lindbergh trial, Bruno Hauptmann repeatedly denied that he was the kidnapper.*

***We* or *us* before a noun** When deciding whether *we* or *us* should precede a noun, choose the pronoun that would be appropriate if the noun were omitted.

    We
▶   ~~Us~~ tenants would rather fight than move.
   ^

    Test: *We would rather fight* [not *Us would rather fight*].

                                     us
▶   Management is shortchanging ~~we~~ tenants.
                                  ^

    Test: *Management is shortchanging us* [not *Management is shortchanging we*].

Pronoun after *than* or *as* When a comparison begins with *than* or *as,* your choice of pronoun will depend on your meaning. To test for the correct pronoun, finish the sentence.

                                         I.
▶   My brother is six years older than ~~me.~~
                                  ^

    Test: *older than I* [am].

▶   We respected no other candidate for city council
                        her.
    as much as ~~she.~~
              ^

    Test: *as much as* [we respected] *her.*

Pronoun before or after an infinitive An infinitive is the word *to* followed by a verb. Both subjects and objects of infinitives take the objective case.

                                me
▶   Ms. Wilson asked John and ~~I~~ to drive the senator
    her   ^
    and ~~she~~ to the airport.
      ^

    John and me is the subject and *senator and her* is the object of the infinitive *to drive.*

Pronoun or noun before a gerund If a pronoun modifies a gerund, use the possessive case: *my, our, your, his,
her, its, their.* A gerund is a verb form ending in *-ing* that
functions as a noun.

▶ The chances of ~~you~~ your being hit by lightning are

about two million to one.

Nouns as well as pronouns may modify gerunds. To form
the possessive case of a noun, use an apostrophe and *-s*
(*victim's*) for a singular noun or just an apostrophe (*victims'*) for a plural noun. (See also 34a.)

▶ The old order in France paid a high price for the
~~aristocracy~~ aristocracy's exploiting the lower classes.

27d *Who* vs. *whom*

Who, a subjective-case pronoun, is used for subjects
and subject complements. *Whom*, an objective-case
pronoun, is used for objects. The words *who* and *whom*
appear primarily in subordinate clauses or in questions.

In subordinate clauses When deciding whether to
use *who* or *whom* in a subordinate clause, check for the
word's function within the clause.

▶ He tells that story to ~~whomever~~ whoever will listen.

> *Whoever* is the subject of *will listen.* The entire sub-
> ordinate clause *whoever will listen* is the object of the
> preposition *to.*

▶ You will work with our senior engineers, ~~who~~ whom you

will meet later.

> *Whom* is the direct object of the verb *will meet.* This
> becomes clear if you restructure the clause: *you will meet
> whom later.* Some writers test by substituting *he* for *who*
> and *him* for *whom*: *you will meet him later.*

In questions When deciding whether to use *who* or
whom in a question, check for the word's function
within the question.

Who
▶ ~~Whom~~ was responsible for creating that computer
  ^
virus?

Who is the subject of the verb *was*.

Whom
▶ ~~Who~~ would you nominate for council president?
  ^

Whom is the direct object of the verb *would nominate*.
This becomes clear if you restructure the question: *You
would nominate whom?*

28 Use adjectives and adverbs appropriately.

Adjectives modify nouns or pronouns; adverbs modify
verbs, adjectives, or other adverbs.

Many adverbs are formed by adding *-ly* to adjectives
(*formal, formally*). But don't assume that all words ending in *-ly* are adverbs or that all adverbs end in *-ly*. Some
adjectives end in *-ly* (*lovely, friendly*), and some adverbs
don't (*always, here*). When in doubt, consult a dictionary.

28a Adjectives

Adjectives ordinarily precede the nouns they modify.
But they can also function as subject complements
following linking verbs (usually a form of *be*: *be, am,
is, are, was, were, being, been*). When an adjective functions as a subject complement, it describes the subject.

Justice is *blind*.

Verbs such as *smell, taste, look, appear, grow*, and
feel may also be linking. If the word following one of
these verbs describes the subject, use an adjective; if
the word modifies the verb, use an adverb.

ADJECTIVE   The detective looked *cautious*.

ADVERB   The detective looked *cautiously* for the
                  fingerprints.

Linking verbs usually suggest states of being, not
actions. For example, to look *cautious* suggests the state
of being cautious, whereas to look *cautiously* is to perform an action in a cautious way.

>   *good*
> Lori looked ~~well~~ in her new raincoat.
>   ^

>   *bad*
> All of us on the debate team felt ~~badly~~ about our
>   ^
>
> performance.

The verbs *looked* and *felt* suggest states of being, not actions, so they should be followed by adjectives.

28b Adverbs

Use adverbs to modify verbs, adjectives, and other adverbs. Adverbs usually answer one of these questions: When? Where? How? Why? Under what conditions? How often? To what degree?

Adjectives are often used incorrectly in place of adverbs in casual or nonstandard speech.

> The manager must ensure that the office runs
> *smoothly*   *efficiently.*
> ~~smooth~~ and ~~efficient.~~
> ^   ^

> The chance of recovering any property lost in the
>   *really*
> fire looks ~~real~~ slim.
>   ^

The incorrect use of the adjective *good* in place of the adverb *well* is especially common in casual or nonstandard speech.

>   *well*
> We were delighted that Nomo had done so ~~good~~
>   ^
>
> on the exam.

28c Comparatives and superlatives

Most adjectives and adverbs have three forms: the positive, the comparative, and the superlative.

POSITIVE	COMPARATIVE	SUPERLATIVE
soft	softer	softest
fast	faster	fastest
careful	more careful	most careful
bad	worse	worst
good	better	best

Comparative vs. superlative   Use the comparative to compare two things, the superlative to compare three or more.

▶ Which of these two brands of toothpaste is ~~best?~~ _better?_

▶ Jia is the ~~more~~ _most_ qualified of the three applicants.

Forms of comparatives and superlatives   To form comparatives and superlatives of one-syllable adjectives, use the endings *-er* and *-est*: *smooth, smoother, smoothest*. For adjectives with three or more syllables, use *more* and *most* (or *less* and *least*): *exciting, more exciting, most exciting*. Two-syllable adjectives form comparatives and superlatives in both ways: *lovely, lovelier, loveliest; helpful, more helpful, most helpful*.

Some one-syllable adverbs take the endings *-er* and *-est* (*fast, faster, fastest*), but longer adverbs and all of those ending in *-ly* use *more* and *most* or *less* and *least* (*carefully, less carefully, least carefully*).

Double comparatives or superlatives   When you have added *-er* or *-est* to an adjective or an adverb, do not also use *more* or *most* (or *less* or *least*).

▶ All the polls indicated that Gore was more ~~likelier~~ _likely_

    to win than Bush.

Absolute concepts   Do not use comparatives or superlatives with absolute concepts such as *unique* or *perfect*. Either something is unique or it isn't. It is illogical to suggest that absolute concepts come in degrees.

▶ That is the most ~~unique~~ _unusual_ wedding gown I have

    ever seen.

29   Repair sentence fragments.

As a rule, do not treat a piece of a sentence as if it were a sentence. When you do, you create a fragment. To be a sentence, a word group must consist of at least one full independent clause. An independent clause includes a subject and a verb, and it either stands alone as a sentence or could stand alone.

You can repair a fragment in one of two ways: Either pull the fragment into a nearby sentence, punctuating the new sentence correctly, or rewrite the fragment as a complete sentence.

29a Fragmented clauses

A subordinate clause is patterned like a sentence, with both a subject and a verb, but it begins with a word that tells readers it cannot stand alone—a word such as *after, although, because, before, if, so that, that, though, unless, until, when, where, which,* or *who.* (For a longer list, see p. 245.)

Most fragmented clauses beg to be pulled into a sentence nearby.

▶ We fear the Zika virus/ ~~Because~~ *because* it is transmitted by

the common mosquito.

If a fragmented clause cannot be attached to a nearby sentence, try rewriting it. The simplest way to turn a fragmented clause into a sentence is to delete the opening word or words that mark it as subordinate.

▶ Uncontrolled development is taking a deadly toll

on the environment. ~~So that in~~ *In* many parts of the

world, fragile ecosystems are collapsing.

29b Fragmented phrases

Like subordinate clauses, certain phrases are sometimes mistaken for sentences. They are fragments if they lack a subject, a verb, or both. Often a fragmented phrase may simply be pulled into a nearby sentence.

▶ The archaeologists worked slowly/, ~~Examining~~ *examining* and

labeling hundreds of pottery shards.

The word group beginning with *Examining* is a verbal phrase, not a sentence.

▶ Many adults suffer silently from agoraphobia/. A ^a^
  fear of the outside world.

> *A fear of the outside world* is an appositive phrase, not a
> sentence.

▶ It has been said that there are only three indigenous
  American art forms/: ~~Jazz,~~ ^jazz,^ musical comedy, and
  soap operas.

> The list is not a sentence. Notice how easily a colon
> corrects the problem. (See 33b.)

If the fragmented phrase cannot be attached to a
nearby sentence, turn the phrase into a sentence. You
may need to add a subject, a verb, or both.

▶ Jamie explained how to access the database. ~~Also~~ ^She also taught us^
  how to submit reports and request vendor payments.

> The revision turns the fragmented phrase into a sentence
> by adding a subject and a verb.

29c Acceptable fragments

Skilled writers occasionally use sentence fragments for
emphasis. Although fragments are sometimes appropriate, writers and readers do not always agree on when
they are appropriate. Therefore, you will find it safer to
write in complete sentences.

30 Revise run-on sentences.

Run-on sentences are independent clauses that have
not been joined correctly. An independent clause is a
word group that can stand alone as a sentence. When
two or more independent clauses appear in one sentence, they must be joined in one of these ways:

- with a comma and a coordinating conjunction
  (*and, but, or, nor, for, so, yet*)
- with a semicolon (or occasionally a colon or a dash)

There are two types of run-on sentences. When a writer puts no mark of punctuation and no coordinating conjunction between independent clauses, the result is a *fused sentence*.

FUSED

Air pollution poses risks to all humans it can be deadly for people with asthma.

A far more common type of run-on sentence is the *comma splice*—two or more independent clauses joined with a comma but without a coordinating conjunction. In some comma splices, the comma appears alone.

COMMA SPLICE

Air pollution poses risks to all humans, it can be deadly for people with asthma.

In other comma splices, the comma is accompanied by a joining word, such as *however*, that is not a coordinating conjunction. (See 30b.)

COMMA SPLICE

Air pollution poses risks to all humans, however, it can be deadly for people with asthma.

To correct a run-on sentence, you have four choices:

1. Use a comma and a coordinating conjunction.
2. Use a semicolon (or, if appropriate, a colon or a dash).
3. Make the clauses into separate sentences.
4. Restructure the sentence, perhaps by subordinating one of the clauses.

CORRECTED WITH COMMA AND COORDINATING CONJUNCTION

Air pollution poses risks to all humans, but it can be deadly for people with asthma.

CORRECTED WITH SEMICOLON

Air pollution poses risks to all humans; it can be deadly for people with asthma.

CORRECTED WITH SEPARATE SENTENCES

Air pollution poses risks to all humans. It can be deadly for people with asthma.

CORRECTED BY RESTRUCTURING

Although air pollution poses risks to all humans, it can be deadly for people with asthma.

One of these revision techniques will usually work better than the others for a particular sentence. The fourth technique, the one requiring the most extensive revision, is often the most effective.

30a Revision with a comma and a coordinating conjunction

When a coordinating conjunction (*and, but, or, nor, for, so, yet*) joins independent clauses, it is usually preceded by a comma.

▶ Most of his friends had made plans for their
retirement, but Tom had not.

30b Revision with a semicolon (or a colon or a dash)

When the independent clauses are closely related and their relation is clear without a coordinating conjunction, a semicolon is an acceptable method of revision.

▶ Tragedy depicts the individual confronted with
the fact of death; comedy depicts the adaptability
of human society.

A semicolon is required between independent clauses that have been linked with a conjunctive adverb such as *however* or *therefore* or a transitional phrase such as *in fact* or *on the contrary*. (See 33a for longer lists.)

▶ The timber wolf looks like a large German shepherd;
however, the wolf has longer legs, larger feet, and a
wider head.

If the first independent clause introduces a quoted sentence, use a colon.

▶ Scholar and crime writer Carolyn Heilbrun

says this about the future/: "Today's shocks are
                       ^

tomorrow's conventions."

Either a colon or a dash may be appropriate when
the second clause summarizes or explains the first. (See
33b and 36d.)

30c Revision by separating sentences

If both independent clauses are long—or if one is a
question and the other is not—consider making them
separate sentences.

▶   ?
Why should we spend money on space exploration/
We   ^
we have enough underfunded programs here on
^
Earth.

30d Revision by restructuring the sentence

For sentence variety, consider restructuring the run-on
sentence, perhaps by turning one of the independent
clauses into a subordinate clause or a phrase.

▶ One of the most famous advertising slogans is

                                   which
Wheaties cereal's "Breakfast of Champions," it
                                            ^
was penned in 1933.

▶ Mary McLeod Bethune, was the 17th child of
                     ^
former slaves, she founded the National Council

of Negro Women in 1935.

31 Consider grammar topics for multilingual writers.

31a Verbs

This section offers a brief review of English verb forms
and tenses and the passive voice.

Verb forms Every main verb in English has five forms (except *be*, which has eight). These forms are used to create all of the verb tenses in Standard English. The following list shows these forms for the regular verb *help* and the irregular verbs *give* and *be*.

	REGULAR (*HELP*)	IRREGULAR (*GIVE*)	IRREGULAR (*BE*)*
BASE FORM	help	give	be
PAST TENSE	helped	gave	was, were
PAST PARTICIPLE	helped	given	been
PRESENT PARTICIPLE	helping	giving	being
***-S* FORM**	helps	gives	is

*Be also has the forms *am* and *are*, which are used in the present tense. (See also 26b.)

Verb tense Here are descriptions of the tenses and progressive forms in Standard English. See also 26b.

The simple tenses show general facts, states of being, and actions that occur regularly.

Simple present tense (base form or *-s* form) expresses general facts, constant states, habitual or repetitive actions, or scheduled future events: *The sun rises in the east. The plane leaves tomorrow at 6:30.*

Simple past tense (base form + *-ed* or *-d* or irregular form) is used for actions that happened at a specific time or during a specific period in the past or for repetitive actions that have ended: *She drove to Montana three years ago. When I was young, I walked to school.*

Simple future tense (*will* + base form) expresses actions that will occur at some time in the future and promises or predictions of future events: *I will call you next week.*

The simple progressive forms show continuing action.

Present progressive (*am, is, are* + present participle) shows actions in progress that are not expected to remain constant or future actions (with verbs such as *go, come,* or *move*): *We are building our house at the shore. They are moving tomorrow.*

Past progressive (*was, were* + present participle) shows actions in progress at a specific past time or a continuing action that was interrupted: *Roy was driving his new car yesterday. When she walked in, we were planning her party.*

Future progressive (*will* + *be* + present participle) expresses actions that will be in progress at a certain time in the future: *Nan will be flying home tomorrow.*

TIP: Certain verbs are not normally used in the progressive: *appear, believe, belong, contain, have, hear, know, like, need, see, seem, taste, think, understand,* and *want.* There are exceptions, however, that you must notice as you encounter them: *We are thinking of buying a summer home.*

The perfect tenses show actions that happened or will happen before another time.

Present perfect tense (*have, has* + past participle) expresses actions that began in the past and continue to the present or actions that happened at an unspecific time in the past: *She has not spoken of her grandfather in a long time. They have traveled to Africa twice.*

Past perfect tense (*had* + past participle) expresses an action that began or occurred before another time in the past: *By the time Hakan was 15, he had learned to drive. I had just finished my walk when my brother drove up.*

Future perfect tense (*will* + *have* + past participle) expresses actions that will be completed before or at a specific future time: *By the time I graduate, I will have taken five film study classes.*

The perfect progressive forms show continuous past actions before another present or past time.

Present perfect progressive (*have, has* + *been* + present participle) expresses continuous actions that began in the past and continue to the present: *My sister has been living in Oregon since 2008.*

Past perfect progressive (*had* + *been* + present participle) conveys actions that began and continued in the past until some other past action: *By the time I moved to Georgia, I had been supporting myself for five years.*

Future perfect progressive (*will* + *have* + *been* + present participle) expresses actions that are or will be in progress before another specified time in the future: *By the* *time we reach the cashier, we will have been waiting in line for an hour.*

Modal verbs The nine modal verbs—*can, could, may, might, must, shall, should, will,* and *would*—are used with the base form of verbs to show certainty, necessity, or possibility. Modals do not change form to indicate tense.

▶ The art museum will ~~launches~~ its fundraising

          launch

   campaign next month.

▶ We could ~~spoke~~ Portuguese when we were young.

     speak

Passive voice When a sentence is written in the passive voice, the subject receives the action instead of doing it. To form the passive voice, use a form of *be*—*am, is, are, was, were, being, be,* or *been*—followed by the past participle of the main verb. (For appropriate uses of the passive voice, see 17b.)

▶ *Dreaming in Cuban* was ~~writing~~ by Cristina García.

              written

▶ Senator Dixon will defeated.

          be

NOTE: Verbs that do not take direct objects—such as *occur, happen, sleep, die,* and *fall*—do not form the passive voice.

31b Articles (*a, an, the*)

Articles and other noun markers Articles (*a, an, the*) are part of a category of words known as *noun markers* or *determiners*. Noun markers identify the nouns that follow them. Besides articles, noun markers include possessive nouns (*Elena's, child's*); possessive pronoun/adjectives (*my, your, their*); demonstrative pronoun/adjectives (*this, that*); quantifiers (*all, few, neither, some*); and numbers (*one, 26*).

        ART N

Felix is reading a book about mythology.

        ART ADJ   N

We took an exciting trip to Alaska last summer.

When to use *a* or *an* Use *a* or *an* with singular count nouns that refer to one unspecific item (not a whole category). *Count nouns* refer to persons, places, things, or ideas that can be counted: *one girl*, *two girls*; *one city*, *three cities*; *one goose*, *four geese*.

▶ My professor asked me to bring ^a^ dictionary to class.

▶ We want to rent ^an^ apartment close to the lake.

When to use *the*   Use *the* with most nouns that the reader can identify specifically. Usually the identity will be clear to the reader for one of the following reasons.

1. The noun has been previously mentioned.

▶ A truck cut in front of our van. When ^the^ truck skidded a few seconds later, we almost crashed into it.

2. A phrase or clause following the noun restricts its identity.

▶ Bryce warned me that ^the^ GPS in his car was not working.

3. A superlative adjective such as *best* or *most intelligent* makes the noun's identity specific. (See also 28c.)

▶ Brita had ^the^ best players on her team.

4. The noun describes a unique person, place, or thing.

▶ During an eclipse, one should not look directly at ^the^ sun.

5. The context or situation makes the noun's identity clear.

▶ Please don't slam ^the^ door when you leave.

6. The noun is singular and refers to a class or category of items (most often animals, musical instruments, or inventions).

▶ ~~Tin~~ The tin whistle is common in traditional Irish music.

When not to use articles   Do not use *a* or *an* with noncount nouns. *Noncount nouns* refer to things or abstract ideas that cannot be counted or made plural: *salt, silver, air, furniture, patience, knowledge.* (See the chart at the bottom of this page.)

To express an approximate amount of a noncount noun, use a quantifier such as *some* or *more*: *some water, enough coffee, less violence.*

▶   Ava gave us ~~an~~ information about the Peace Corps.

▶   Claudia said she had <del>a</del> *some* news that would surprise

her parents.

Do not use articles with nouns that refer to all of something or something in general.

▶   *Kindness*
   ~~The kindness~~ is a virtue.

▶   In some parts of the world, ~~the~~ rice is preferred to

all other grains.

Commonly used noncount nouns

Food and drink

beef, bread, butter, candy, cereal, cheese, cream, meat, milk, pasta, rice, salt, sugar, wine

Nonfood substances

air, cement, coal, dirt, gasoline, gold, paper, petroleum, plastic, rain, silver, snow, soap, steel, wood, wool

Abstract nouns

advice, anger, beauty, confidence, courage, employment, fun, happiness, health, honesty, information, intelligence, knowledge, love, poverty, satisfaction, wealth

Other

biology (and other areas of study), clothing, equipment, furniture, homework, jewelry, luggage, machinery, mail, money, news, poetry, pollution, research, scenery, traffic, transportation, violence, weather, work

NOTE: A few noncount nouns can also be used as count nouns: *He had two loves: music and archery.*

When to use articles with proper nouns   Do not use articles with most singular proper nouns: *Prime Minister Trudeau, Jamaica, Lake Huron, Ivy Street, Mount Everest.* Use *the* with most plural proper nouns: *the McGregors, the Bahamas, the Finger Lakes, the United States.* Also use *the* with large regions, oceans, rivers, and mountain ranges: *the Sahara, the Indian Ocean, the Amazon River, the Rocky Mountains.*

There are, however, many exceptions, especially with geographic names. Note exceptions when you encounter them or consult a native speaker or an ESL dictionary.

31c Sentence structure

This section focuses on the major challenges that multilingual students face when writing sentences in English.

Omitted verbs   Some languages do not use linking verbs (*am, is, are, was, were*) between subjects and complements (nouns or adjectives that rename or describe the subject). Every English sentence, however, must include a verb.

▶   Jim $\overset{is}{\wedge}$ intelligent.

▶   Many streets in San Francisco $\overset{are}{\wedge}$ very steep.

Omitted subjects   Some languages do not require a subject in every sentence. Every English sentence, however, needs a subject.

▶   Your aunt is very energetic. $\overset{She\ seems}{\wedge}$ ~~Seems~~ young for her age.

EXCEPTION: In commands, the subject *you* is understood but not present in the sentence: *Give me the book.*

The word *it* is used as the subject of a sentence describing the weather or temperature, stating the time, indicating distance, or suggesting an environmental fact. Do not omit *it* in such sentences.

It is raining in the valley and snowing in the mountains.

It is 9:15 a.m.

It is three hundred miles to Chicago.

In July, *it* is very hot in Arizona.

In some English sentences, the subject comes after the verb, and a placeholder (called an expletive)—*there* or *it*—comes before the verb.

EXP V ┌──── S ────┐   ┌──── S ────┐ V
There are many people here today. (Many people are here today.)

EXP V   ┌─ S ─┐   ┌─ S ─┐   V
It is important to study daily. (To study daily is important.)

                    there are
▶ **As you know, ⌄ many religious sects in India.**

Repeated subjects, objects, and adverbs   English does not allow a subject to be repeated in its own clause.

▶ **The doctor ~~she~~ advised me to cut down on salt.**

Do not add a pronoun even when a word group comes between the subject and the verb.

▶ **The car that had been stolen ~~it~~ was found.**

Do not repeat an object or an adverb in an adjective clause. Adjective clauses begin with relative pronouns (*who, whom, whose, which, that*) or relative adverbs (*when, where*). Relative pronouns usually serve as subjects or objects in the clauses they introduce; another word in the clause cannot serve the same function. Relative adverbs should not be repeated by other adverbs later in the clause.

▶ **The cat ran under the car that ~~it~~ was parked on**

the street.

The relative pronoun *that* is the subject of the adjective clause, so the pronoun *it* cannot be added as the subject.

If the clause begins with a relative adverb, do not use another adverb with the same meaning later in the clause.

▶ **The office where I work ~~there~~ is close to home.**

The adverb *there* cannot repeat the relative adverb *where*.

31d Prepositions showing time and place

The chart on this page is limited to three prepositions that show time and place: *at*, *on*, and *in*. Not every possible use is listed in the chart, so don't be surprised when you encounter exceptions and idiomatic uses that you must learn one at a time. For example, in English, we ride *in* a car but *on* a bus, plane, train, or subway.

At, *on*, and *in* to show time and place

Showing time

AT *at* a specific time: *at* 7:20, *at* dawn, *at* dinner

ON *on* a specific day or date: *on* Tuesday, *on* June 4

IN *in* a part of a day: *in* the afternoon, *in* the daytime [but *at* night]

  in a year or month: *in* 1999, *in* July

  in a period of time: finished *in* three hours

Showing place

AT *at* a meeting place or location: *at* home, *at* the club

  at a specific address: living *at* 10 Oak Street

  at the edge of something: sitting *at* the desk

  at the corner of something: turning *at* the intersection

  at a target: throwing the snowball *at* Lucy

ON *on* a surface: placed *on* the table, hanging *on* the wall

  on a street: the house *on* Spring Street

  on an electronic medium: *on* television, *on* the Internet

IN *in* an enclosed space: *in* the garage, *in* an envelope

  in a geographic location: *in* San Diego, *in* Texas

  in a print medium: *in* a book, *in* a magazine

Punctuation

32 The comma

The comma was invented to help readers. Without it, sentence parts can collide into one another unexpectedly, causing misreadings.

CONFUSING If you cook Elmer will do the dishes.

CONFUSING While we were eating a rattlesnake approached our campsite.

Add commas in the logical places (after *cook* and *eating*), and suddenly all is clear. No longer is Elmer being cooked, or the rattlesnake being eaten.

Various rules have evolved to prevent such misreadings and to guide readers through complex grammatical structures. Those rules are detailed in sections 32a–32i. (Section 32j explains when not to use a comma.)

32a Before a coordinating conjunction joining independent clauses

When a coordinating conjunction connects two or more independent clauses—word groups that could stand alone as separate sentences—a comma must come before the conjunction. There are seven coordinating conjunctions in English: *and, but, or, nor, for, so,* and *yet.*

A comma tells readers that one independent clause has come to a close and that another is about to begin.

▶ Respondents were given 5 minutes, but none
                                      ^
completed the survey.

EXCEPTION: If the two independent clauses are short and there is no danger of misreading, the comma may be left out.

The plane took off and we were on our way.

TIP: As a rule, do *not* use a comma with a coordinating conjunction that joins only two words, phrases, or subordinate clauses. (See 32j. See also 32c for commas with coordinating conjunctions joining three or more elements.)

32b After an introductory word group

Use a comma after an introductory clause or phrase. A comma tells readers that the introductory word group has come to a close and that the main part of the sentence is about to begin. The most common introductory word groups are adverb clauses, prepositional phrases, and participial phrases.

▶ **When Karl Marx wrote *Das Kapital*, many societies were in the early stages of industrialization.**

▶ **During the past decade, scientists have made important discoveries about how humans form memories.**

▶ **Buried under layers of younger rocks, the earth's oldest rocks contain no fossils.**

EXCEPTION: The comma may be omitted after a short clause or phrase if there is no danger of misreading.

In no time we were at 2,800 feet.

NOTE: Other introductory word groups include transitional expressions and absolute phrases (see 32f).

32c Between items in a series

In a series of three or more items (words, phrases, or clauses), use a comma between all items, including the last two.

▶ **Concentrated poverty, high rates of unemployment, high crime rates, and social disorder are common in the precinct.**

32d Between coordinate adjectives

Use a comma between coordinate adjectives, those that each modify a noun separately.

▶ Should patients with severe, irreversible brain

damage be put on life support systems?

Adjectives that can be connected with *and* are coordinate: *severe and irreversible*.

NOTE: Do not use a comma between cumulative adjectives, those that do not each modify the noun separately.

> *Three large gray* shapes moved slowly toward us.

Cumulative adjectives cannot be joined with *and* (not *three and large and gray shapes*).

32e To set off a nonrestrictive element, but not a restrictive element

A *restrictive* element defines or limits the meaning of the word it modifies; it is therefore essential to the meaning of the sentence and is not set off with commas. A *nonrestrictive* element describes a word whose meaning is clear without it. Because it is not essential to the meaning of the sentence, it is set off with commas.

RESTRICTIVE (NO COMMAS)

Adolescents need activities *that are positive.*

NONRESTRICTIVE (WITH COMMAS)

Adolescents need positive activities, *which do not have to be expensive.*

If you remove a restrictive element from a sentence, the meaning changes significantly, becoming more general than intended. The writer of the first sample sentence is not saying that adolescents need activities in general. The meaning is more restricted: Adolescents need *positive* activities.

If you remove a nonrestrictive element from a sentence, the meaning does not change significantly. Some information may be lost, but the defining characteristics of the person or thing described remain the same: Adolescents need *positive activities*, and these need not be expensive.

Elements that may be restrictive or nonrestrictive include adjective clauses, adjective phrases, and appositives.

32e

Adjective clauses   Adjective clauses, which usually follow the noun or pronoun they describe, begin with a relative pronoun (*who, whom, whose, which, that*) or with a relative adverb (*when, where*). When an adjective clause is nonrestrictive, set it off with commas; when it is restrictive, omit the commas.

NONRESTRICTIVE CLAUSE (WITH COMMAS)

▶   The Kyoto Protocol, which was adopted in 1997,

aims to reduce greenhouse gases.

RESTRICTIVE CLAUSE (NO COMMAS)

▶   The giant panda/that was born at the San Diego

Zoo in 2003/was sent to China in 2007.

NOTE: Use *that* only with restrictive clauses. Many writers use *which* only with nonrestrictive clauses, but usage varies.

Adjective phrases   Prepositional or verbal phrases functioning as adjectives may be restrictive or nonrestrictive. Nonrestrictive phrases are set off with commas; restrictive phrases are not.

NONRESTRICTIVE PHRASE (WITH COMMAS)

▶   The eight students, with their lab kits in hand,

began the experiment.

RESTRICTIVE PHRASE (NO COMMAS)

▶   One corner of the attic was filled with newspapers/

dating from the 1920s.

Appositives   An appositive is a noun or pronoun that renames a nearby noun. Nonrestrictive appositives are set off with commas; restrictive appositives are not.

NONRESTRICTIVE APPOSITIVE (WITH COMMAS)

▶   Darwin's most important book, *On the Origin of*

Species, was the result of many years of research.

RESTRICTIVE APPOSITIVE (NO COMMAS)

▶ Selections from the book/*Democracy and Education*/

were read aloud in class.

32f To set off transitional and parenthetical expressions, absolute phrases, and word groups expressing contrast

Transitional expressions Transitional expressions serve as bridges between sentences or parts of sentences. They include conjunctive adverbs such as *however*, *therefore*, and *moreover* and transitional phrases such as *for example* and *as a matter of fact*. For more examples, see 33a.

When a transitional expression appears between independent clauses in a compound sentence, it is preceded by a semicolon and usually followed by a comma.

▶ Minh did not understand our language; moreover,
                                                    ∧

he was unfamiliar with our customs.

When a transitional expression appears at the beginning of a sentence or in the middle of an independent clause, it is usually set off with commas.

▶ In fact, stock values rose after the company's press
      ∧

release.

▶ Natural foods are not always salt-free; celery, for
                                                       ∧

example, is relatively high in sodium.
         ∧

Parenthetical expressions Expressions that provide only supplemental information and interrupt the flow of a sentence should be set off with commas.

▶ Evolution, so far as we know, doesn't work this way.
          ∧   ∧

Absolute phrases An absolute phrase consists of a noun followed by a participle or participial phrase. It modifies the whole sentence and should be set off with commas.

```
┌──────── ABSOLUTE PHRASE ────────┐
         N PARTICIPLE
```
The sun appearing for the first time all week, we were

at last able to begin the archaeological dig.

Word groups expressing contrast   Sharp contrasts beginning with words such as *not* and *unlike* are set off with commas.

▶   Unlike Robert, Celia loved poetry slams.
             ^

32g To set off nouns of direct address, the words *yes* and *no*, interrogative tags, and mild interjections

▶   Forgive me, Angela, for forgetting our meeting.
            ^   ^

▶   Yes, the loan will probably be approved.
       ^

▶   The film was faithful to the book, wasn't it?
                                    ^

▶   Well, cases like this are difficult to decide.
        ^

32h To set off direct quotations introduced with expressions such as *he said*

▶   Gladwell asserts, "Those who are successful . . .
                   ^

are most likely to be given the kinds of special

opportunities that lead to further success" (30).

32i With dates, addresses, and titles

Dates   In dates, set off the year from the rest of the sentence with a pair of commas.

▶   On December 12, 1890, orders were sent out for
                 ^   ^

the arrest of Sitting Bull.

EXCEPTIONS: Commas are not needed if the date is inverted or if only the month and year are given: *The 15 April 2018 deadline is approaching. May 2016 was a surprisingly cold month.*

Addresses   The elements of an address or a place name are separated by commas. A zip code, however, is not preceded by a comma.

▶   The teen group met at 708 Spring Street, Washington,
                                          ∧   ∧
IL 61571.

Titles   If a title follows a name, set off the title with a pair of commas.

▶   Sandra Barnes, MD, was appointed to the board.
                        ∧   ∧

32j Misuses of the comma

Do not use commas unless you have good reasons for using them. In particular, avoid using commas in the following situations.

WITH A COORDINATING CONJUNCTION JOINING ONLY TWO WORDS, PHRASES, OR SUBORDINATE CLAUSES

▶   Marie Curie discovered radium/ and later applied her work on radioactivity to medicine.

TO SEPARATE A VERB FROM ITS SUBJECT

▶   Zoos large enough to give the animals freedom to roam/ are becoming more popular.

BETWEEN CUMULATIVE ADJECTIVES (See 32c.)

▶   We found an old/ maroon hatbox.

TO SET OFF RESTRICTIVE ELEMENTS (See 32e.)

▶   Drivers/ who think they own the road/ make cycling a dangerous sport.

▶   Margaret Mead's book/ *Coming of Age in Samoa*/ caused controversy when it was published.

AFTER A COORDINATING CONJUNCTION

▶   TV talk shows are sometimes performed live, but/ more often they are taped.

AFTER *SUCH AS* OR *LIKE*

▶ Bacterial infections such as/methicillin-resistant
Staphylococcus aureus (MRSA) have become a
serious concern in hospitals.

BEFORE *THAN*

▶ Touring Crete was more thrilling for us/than
visiting the Greek islands frequented by the rich.

BEFORE A PARENTHESIS

▶ At InterComm, Sylvia began at the bottom/(with
only a cubicle and a swivel chair), but within
three years she had been promoted to supervisor.

TO SET OFF AN INDIRECT (REPORTED) QUOTATION

▶ Samuel Goldwyn once said/that a verbal contract
isn't worth the paper it's written on.

WITH A QUESTION MARK OR AN EXCLAMATION POINT

▶ "Why don't you try it?/" she coaxed.

33 The semicolon and the colon

33a The semicolon

The semicolon is used between independent clauses
not joined with a coordinating conjunction. It can also
be used between items in a series containing internal
punctuation.

The semicolon is never used between elements of
unequal grammatical rank.

Between independent clauses When two independent clauses appear in one sentence, they are usually
linked with a comma and a coordinating conjunction

(*and, but, or, nor, for, so, yet*). The coordinating conjunction signals the relation between the clauses. If the relation is clear without a conjunction, a writer may choose to connect the clauses with a semicolon instead.

> In film, a low-angle shot makes the subject look powerful; a high-angle shot does just the opposite.

A writer may also connect the clauses with a semicolon and a conjunctive adverb such as *however* or a transitional phrase such as *for example.*

> Many corals grow very gradually; in fact, the creation of a coral reef can take centuries.

CONJUNCTIVE ADVERBS

accordingly, also, anyway, besides, certainly, consequently, conversely, finally, furthermore, hence, however, incidentally, indeed, instead, likewise, meanwhile, moreover, nevertheless, next, nonetheless, now, otherwise, similarly, specifically, still, subsequently, then, therefore, thus

TRANSITIONAL PHRASES

after all, as a matter of fact, as a result, at any rate, at the same time, even so, for example, for instance, in addition, in conclusion, in fact, in other words, in the first place, on the contrary

NOTE: A semicolon must be used whenever a coordinating conjunction does not appear between independent clauses. To use merely a comma—or to use a comma and a conjunctive adverb or transitional expression—creates an error known as a *comma splice.* (See 30.)

Between items in a series containing internal punctuation Three or more items in a series are usually separated by commas. If one or more of the items contain internal punctuation, a writer may use semicolons for clarity.

> Science suggests that you can improve your memory by sleeping seven to eight hours a day; using mnemonics, self-testing, and visualization techniques; and including water, berries, and fish in your diet.

Misuses of the semicolon Do not use a semicolon in the following situations.

33b

BETWEEN AN INDEPENDENT CLAUSE AND A SUBORDINATE CLAUSE

▶ The media like to portray my generation as lazy~~;~~, although polls show that we work as hard as the twenty somethings before us.

BETWEEN AN APPOSITIVE AND THE WORD IT REFERS TO

▶ We were fascinated by the species *Argyroneta aquatica*~~;~~, a spider that lives underwater.

TO INTRODUCE A LIST

▶ Some public sector professions require specialized training~~;~~: teaching, law enforcement, and firefighting.

BETWEEN INDEPENDENT CLAUSES JOINED BY *AND*, *BUT*, *OR*, *NOR*, *FOR*, *SO*, OR *YET*

▶ Five of the applicants had used spreadsheets~~;~~, but only one was familiar with databases.

33b The colon

Main uses of the colon   A colon can be used after an independent clause to direct readers' attention to a list, an appositive, or a quotation.

A LIST

The routine includes the following: 20 knee bends, 50 leg lifts, and 5 minutes of running in place.

AN APPOSITIVE

My roommate lives on two things: snacks and social media.

A QUOTATION

Consider the words of Benjamin Franklin: "There never was a good war or a bad peace."

For other ways of introducing quotations, see 35c.

A colon may also be used between independent clauses if the second clause summarizes or explains the first clause.

Faith is like love: It cannot be forced.

When an independent clause follows a colon, begin the independent clause with a capital letter. (See 37f.)

Conventional uses   Use a colon after the salutation in a formal letter, to indicate hours and minutes, to show proportions, between a title and a subtitle, to separate location and publisher in reference list entries, and between chapter and verse in citations of sacred texts.

Dear Editor:

5:30 p.m.

The ratio of women to men was 2:1.

Alvin Ailey: A Life in Dance

Boston, MA: Bedford/St. Martin's

Luke 2:14, Qur'an 67:3

Misuses of the colon   A colon must be preceded by an independent clause. Therefore, avoid using it in the following situations.

BETWEEN A VERB AND ITS OBJECT OR COMPLEMENT

▶ Some important vitamins found in vegetables are:̸

vitamin A, thiamine, niacin, and vitamin C.

BETWEEN A PREPOSITION AND ITS OBJECT

▶ The heart's two pumps each consist of:̸ an upper

chamber, or atrium, and a lower chamber, or

ventricle.

AFTER *SUCH AS, INCLUDING*, OR *FOR EXAMPLE*

▶ The NCAA regulates college sports, including:̸

basketball, softball, and football.

34 The apostrophe

The apostrophe indicates possession and marks contractions. In addition, it has a few conventional uses.

34a To indicate possession

The apostrophe is used to indicate that a noun or an indefinite pronoun is possessive. Possessives usually indicate ownership, as in *Tim's hat, the writer's desk,* or *someone's gloves.* Frequently, however, ownership is only loosely implied: *the tree's roots, a day's work.* If you are not sure whether a word is possessive, try turning it into an *of* phrase: *the roots of the tree, the work of a day.*

When to add -'s   Add -'s if the noun does not end in -*s* or if the noun is singular and ends in -*s* or an *s* sound.

> Luck often propels a rock musician's career.

> Thank you for refunding the children's money.

> Lois's sister spent last year in India.

> Her article presents an overview of Marx's teachings.

EXCEPTION: If pronunciation would be awkward with an apostrophe and an -*s*, some writers use only the apostrophe: *Sophocles'.*

When to add only an apostrophe   If the noun is plural and ends in -*s*, add only an apostrophe.

> Both diplomats' briefcases were searched by guards.

Joint possession   To show joint possession, use -'s (or -*s'*) with the last noun only; to show individual possession, make all nouns possessive.

> Have you seen Joyce and Greg's new camper?

> Hernando's and Maria's expectations were quite different.

Compound nouns   If a noun is compound, use -'s (or -*s'*) with the last element.

> Her father-in-law's sculpture won first place.

Indefinite pronouns such as someone Use -'s to indicate that an indefinite pronoun is possessive. Indefinite pronouns refer to no specific person or thing: *anyone*, *everyone*, *someone*, *no one*, and so on.

This diet will improve almost anyone's health.

NOTE: Possessive pronouns (*its*, *his*, and so on) do not use an apostrophe. (See 34d.)

34b To mark contractions

In a contraction, an apostrophe takes the place of missing letters.

It's unfortunate that many children can't get the services they need.

It's stands for *it is*, *can't* for *cannot*.
The apostrophe is also used to mark the omission of the first two digits of a year (*the class of '13*) or years (*the '60s generation*).

34c Conventional uses

An apostrophe typically is not used to pluralize numbers, abbreviations, letters, or words mentioned as words. Note the few exceptions and be consistent in your writing.

Plural numbers and abbreviations Do not use an apostrophe in the plural of any numbers (including decades) or of any abbreviations.

Peggy skated nearly perfect figure 8s.

DVDs first became available in the 1990s.

Plural letters Italicize the letter and use roman (regular) font style for the -*s* ending.

Two large *J*s were painted on the door.

To avoid misreading, you may use an apostrophe with some letters: *A*'s.

Plural of words mentioned as words Italicize the word and use roman (regular) font style for the -*s* ending.

We've heard enough *maybe*s.

34d Misuses of the apostrophe

Do not use an apostrophe in the following situations.

WITH NOUNS THAT ARE PLURAL BUT NOT POSSESSIVE

▶ Some ~~outpatient's~~ outpatients have special parking permits.

IN THE POSSESSIVE PRONOUNS *ITS*, *WHOSE*, *HIS*, *HERS*, *OURS*, *YOURS*, AND *THEIRS*

▶ Each area has ~~it's~~ its own conference room.

▶ We attended a reading by Michael Chabon, ~~who's~~ whose

work often focuses on Jewish identity.

It's means "it is"; *who's* means "who is" (see 34b). Possessive pronouns such as *its* and *whose* contain no apostrophes.

35 Quotation marks

Quotation marks are used to enclose direct quotations. They are also used around some titles.

35a To enclose direct quotations

Direct quotations of a person's words, whether spoken or written, must be in quotation marks.

> "The contract negotiations are stalled," the mediator told reporters, "but I'll bring both sides together."

NOTE: Do not use quotation marks around indirect quotations, which report what a person said without using the person's exact words.

> The mediator pledged to find a compromise even though negotiations had broken down.

Quotation within quotation   Use single quotation marks to enclose a quotation within a quotation.

> Marshall (2006) noted that Elizabeth Peabody wanted her school to focus on "not merely 'teaching' but 'educating children morally and spiritually as well as intellectually from the first'" (p. 107).

Indented (block) quotations   In an APA-style paper, when a long quotation (40 or more words) has been set off from the text by indenting, do not use quotation marks around the quotation. (See 35d.) However, use double quotation marks around quoted words that appear within a block quotation.

A report by the Henry J. Kaiser Family Foundation (2004) outlined trends that may have contributed to the childhood obesity crisis:

> a reduction in physical education classes and after-school athletic programs, an increase in the availability of sodas and snacks in public schools, the growth in the number of fast-food outlets . . . , the trend toward "super-sizing" food portions in restaurants, and the increasing number of highly processed high-calorie and high-fat grocery products. (p. 1)

35b Around titles of short works

Use quotation marks around titles of short works such as articles, poems, short stories, songs, television and radio episodes, and chapters or subdivisions of long works.

> Nirvana's song "All Apologies" is a classic.

NOTE: Titles of long works such as books, plays, television and radio programs, films, magazines, and so on are put in italics. (See 40a.)

35c Other punctuation with quotation marks

This section describes the conventions to observe in placing various marks of punctuation inside or outside quotation marks. It also explains how to punctuate when introducing quoted material.

Periods and commas   Place periods and commas inside quotation marks.

> "I'm here for my service-learning project," I told the teacher. "I'd like to become a reading specialist."

This rule applies to single and double quotation marks, and it applies to quotation marks around words, phrases, and clauses.

EXCEPTION: In parenthetical in-text citations, the period follows the citation in parentheses: *According to Cole (1999), "The instruments of science have vastly extended our senses" (p. 53).*

Colons and semicolons   Put colons and semicolons outside quotation marks.

> Harold wrote, "I regret that I cannot attend the fundraiser for AIDS research"; his letter, however, contained a contribution.

Question marks and exclamation points   Put question marks and exclamation points inside quotation marks unless they apply to the whole sentence.

> Professor Abrams asked us on the first day of class, "What are your three goals for the course?"

> Have you heard the old proverb "Do not climb the hill until you reach it"?

In the first sentence, the question mark applies only to the quoted question. In the second sentence, the question mark applies to the whole sentence.

Introducing quoted material   After a word group introducing a quotation, choose a colon, a comma, or no punctuation at all, whichever is appropriate in context.

If a quotation has been formally introduced, a colon is appropriate. A formal introduction is a full independent clause, not just an expression such as *he said* or *she writes*.

> Friedman (2006) provides a challenging yet optimistic view of the future: "We need to get back to work on our country and on our planet. The hour is late, the stakes couldn't be higher, the project couldn't be harder, the payoff couldn't be greater" (p. 25).

If a quotation is introduced or followed by an expression such as *he said* or *she writes,* use a comma.

> Phillips (1993) claimed, "The idea of the unconscious is, among other things, a way of describing the fact that there are things we didn't know we could say" (p. 25).

> "Unless another war is prevented it is likely to bring destruction on a scale never before held possible,"

Einstein (1947, p. 29) wrote in the aftermath of the atomic bomb.

When you blend a quotation into your own sentence, use either a comma or no punctuation, depending on the way the quotation fits into your sentence structure.

The future champion could, as he put it, "float like a butterfly and sting like a bee."

Woolf (1928) wrote that "a woman must have money and a room of her own if she is to write fiction" (p. 4).

If a quotation appears at the beginning of a sentence, use a comma after it unless the quotation ends with a question mark or an exclamation point.

"I've always thought of myself as a reporter," Brooks stated (1987, p. 162).

"What is it?" she asked, bracing herself.

If a quoted sentence is interrupted by explanatory words, use commas to set off the explanatory words.

"With regard to air travel," Ambrose (1997) noted, "Jefferson was a full century ahead of the curve" (p. 53).

If two successive quoted sentences from the same source are interrupted by explanatory words, use a comma before the explanatory words and a period after them.

"Everyone agrees journalists must tell the truth," Kovach and Rosenstiel (2001) write. "Yet people are befuddled about what 'the truth' means" (p. 37).

35d Misuses of quotation marks

Avoid using quotation marks in the following situations.

FAMILIAR SLANG, TRITE EXPRESSIONS, OR HUMOR

▶ The economist emphasized that 5 percent was a ⫽ballpark figure.⫽

INDIRECT QUOTATIONS

▶ After finishing the exam, Chuck said that ⫽he was due for a coffee break.⫽

36 Other marks

36a The period

Use a period to end all sentences except direct questions or genuine exclamations.

> The therapist asked whether the session was beneficial.

A period is conventionally used with personal titles, Latin abbreviations, and designations for time.

Mr.	i.e.	a.m.
Ms.	e.g.	p.m.
Dr.	etc.	

NOTE: If a sentence ends with a period marking an abbreviation, do not add a second period.

A period is not used for most other abbreviations.

CA	UNESCO	FCC	NATO	BS	cm
NY	AFL-CIO	IRS	USA	PhD	min

36b The question mark

Use a question mark after a direct question.

> Which economists have argued for free markets?

NOTE: Use a period, not a question mark, after an indirect question, one that is reported rather than asked directly.

> He asked me who was teaching the engineering course.

36c The exclamation point

Use an exclamation point after a sentence that expresses exceptional feeling or deserves special emphasis.

> We yelled to the attending physician, "He's not drunk! He's in diabetic shock!"

Do not overuse the exclamation point.

▶ In the fisherman's memory, the fish lives on,

increasing in length and weight each year, until it

is big enough to shade a fishing boat/.
                                      ^

This sentence doesn't need to be pumped up with an exclamation point. It is emphatic enough without it.

36d The dash

The dash may be used to set off parenthetical material that deserves special emphasis. When typing, use two hyphens to form a dash (--), with no spaces before or after the dash. If your word processing program has what is known as an "em-dash" (—), you may use it instead, with no space before or after it.

Use a dash to introduce a list, to signal a restatement or an amplification, or to indicate a striking shift in tone or thought.

> Along the wall are the bulk liquids—sesame seed oil, honey, safflower oil, and half-liquid peanut butter.

> Peter decided to focus on his priorities—applying to graduate school, getting financial aid, and finding a roommate.

> Kiere took a few steps back, came running full speed, kicked a mighty kick—and missed the ball.

In the first two examples, the writer could also use a colon. (See 33b.) The colon is more formal than the dash and not quite as dramatic.

Use a pair of dashes to set off parenthetical material that deserves special emphasis or to set off an appositive that contains commas.

> Everything in the classroom—from the pencils on the desks to the books on the shelves—was in perfect order.

> In my hometown, people's basic needs—food, clothing, and shelter—are less costly than in Denver.

TIP: Unless you have a specific reason for using the dash, avoid it. Unnecessary dashes create a choppy effect.

36e Parentheses

Parentheses have several conventional uses.

Supplemental information   Use parentheses to enclose supplemental material, minor digressions, and afterthoughts.

> Nurses record patients' vital signs (temperature, pulse, and blood pressure) several times a day.

Abbreviations   Use parentheses around an abbreviation following the spelled-out form the first time you mention the term. Use the abbreviation alone in subsequent references.

> Data from the Uniform Crime Reports (UCR) indicate that homicide rates have been declining. Because most murders are reported to the police, the data from the UCR are widely viewed as a valid indicator of homicide rates.

Technical notation   Statistical values, degrees of freedom, and other technical expressions are often enclosed in parentheses.

> The relationship between these variables was statistically significant ($p = .021$).
> $t(80) = 2.22$
> $F(2, 118) = 4.55$

Series   Use parentheses to enclose letters or numbers labeling items in a series.

> Freudians recognize three parts to a person's psyche: (a) the unconscious id, where basic drives such as hunger reside; (b) the ego, which controls many of our conscious decisions; and (c) the superego, which regulates behavior according to internalized societal expectations.

Documentation   Parentheses are used around dates and page numbers in in-text citations and around dates in reference list entries. (See sections 13 and 14.)

Inappropriate use   Do not overuse parentheses. Often a sentence reads more gracefully without them.

▷ Research shows that 17 million ~~(estimates run as~~ ^from^ ^to^ ~~high as~~ 23 million)̷ Americans have diabetes.

36f Brackets

Use brackets to enclose any words or phrases you have inserted into an otherwise word-for-word quotation.

> As Simon (2007) has argued, "Perhaps the most important feature of this change has been an enormous expansion of power [for prosecutors] at the expense of judges, paroling authorities, and defense lawyers" (p. 35).

Simon's book did not contain the words *for prosecutors* in the sentence quoted.

The Latin word *sic* in brackets indicates that an error in a quoted sentence appears in the original source.

> According to the review, the book was "an important contribution to gender studies, suceeding [*sic*] where others have fallen short."

36g The ellipsis mark

Use an ellipsis mark, three spaced periods, to indicate that you have deleted material from an otherwise word-for-word quotation.

> Harmon (2011) noted, "During hibernation, heart rate would drop to nine beats per minute between breaths . . . and then speed up with each inhale."

If you delete a full sentence or more in the middle of a quoted passage, use a period before the three ellipsis dots.

NOTE: Do not use the ellipsis mark at the beginning or end of a quotation unless it is important, for clarity, to indicate that the passage quoted is from the middle of a sentence.

36h The slash

Use the slash to separate two or three lines of poetry that have been run into your text. Add a space both before and after the slash.

> Herbert (1633) poked fun at popular poems of his time: "Who says that fictions only and false hair / Become a verse? Is there in truth no beauty?"

A slash is used in an in-text citation for the dates of a republished work: (1867/2011).

Use the slash sparingly, if at all, to separate options: *pass/fail, producer/director*. Put no space around the slash. Avoid using expressions such as *he/she* and *his/her* and the awkward construction *and/or*.

Mechanics

37 Capitalization

In addition to reading the following guidelines, consult a good dictionary for help in determining when to use capital letters.

37a Proper vs. common nouns

Proper nouns and words derived from them are capitalized; common nouns are not. Proper nouns name specific persons, places, and things. All other nouns are common nouns.

The following types of words are usually capitalized: names of deities, religions, religious followers, and sacred books; words of family relationship used as names; particular places; nationalities and their languages, races, and tribes; educational institutions, departments, and particular courses; government departments, organizations, and political parties; historical movements, periods, events, and documents; and trade names.

PROPER NOUNS	COMMON NOUNS
God (used as a name)	a god
Book of Common Prayer	a sacred book
Uncle Pedro	my uncle
Father (used as a name)	my father
Lake Superior	a large lake
the South	a southern state
Wrigley Field	a baseball stadium
Swedish	a nationality
Pinghua	a dialect
University of Wisconsin	a state university
Geology 101	a geology course
Veterans Administration	a federal agency
Phi Kappa Psi	a fraternity
the Democratic Party	a political party
the Enlightenment	the eighteenth century
Xerox	a photocopy

Months, holidays, and days of the week are capitalized: *May, Labor Day, Monday.* The seasons and numbers of the days of the month are not: *summer, the fifth of June.*

Names of school subjects are capitalized only if they are names of languages: *English, French, geology, history.*

NOTE: Do not capitalize common nouns to make them seem important: *Our company is currently hiring technical support staff* [not *Company, Technical Support Staff*].

37b Titles with proper names

Capitalize a title when used as part of a proper name but usually not when used alone.

> Prof. Margaret Burnes; Dr. Sinyee Sein; John Scott Williams Jr.; Anne Tilton, LLD

> District Attorney Mill was ruled out of order.

> The district attorney was elected for a two-year term.

> Usage varies when the title of a public figure is used alone: *The president* [or *President*] *vetoed the bill.*

37c Titles of works

In titles and subtitles of works mentioned in the text of a paper, capitalize all major words (nouns, pronouns, verbs, adjectives, and adverbs) as well as all words of four letters or more. Minor words of fewer than four characters (articles, prepositions, and coordinating conjunctions) are not capitalized unless they are the first or last word of a title or subtitle.

> *The Impossible Theater: A Manifesto*

> "The Truth About the National Debt"

> *A Guide to Working With Adolescents*

Titles of works are handled differently in the APA reference list. See section 14.

37d Special terms

In the social sciences, the following terms are typically capitalized.

SPECIFIC TITLES OF TESTS   Myers-Briggs Type Indicator

NOUNS FOLLOWED BY LETTERS OR NUMBERS   Type 2 diabetes, Trial 5

TRADE NAMES OF DRUGS   Advil, Benadryl

The following are typically lowercase.

GENERIC TITLES OF TESTS   career preference test

NOUNS FOLLOWED BY VARIABLES   type x, trial y

GENERIC NAMES OF DRUGS   ibuprofen, diphenhydramine

NAMES OF THEORIES   social disorganization theory

NOTE: Terms derived from proper nouns are capitalized:
Marxian economics.

37e First word of a sentence or quoted sentence

The first word of a sentence should be capitalized. Capitalize the first word of a quoted sentence but not a quoted phrase.

> Loveless (2011) wrote, "If failing schools are ever to be turned around, much more must be learned about how schools age as institutions" (p. 25).

> Baker (1967) has written that sports are "the opiate of the masses" (p. 46).

If a quoted sentence is interrupted by explanatory words, do not capitalize the first word after the interruption.

> "When we all think alike," he said, "no one is thinking."

When a sentence appears within parentheses, capitalize the first word unless the parentheses appear within another sentence.

> Early detection of breast cancer increases survival rates. (See Table 2.)

> Early detection of breast cancer increases survival rates (see Table 2).

37f First word following a colon

Capitalize the first word after a colon if it begins an independent clause.

> Suddenly the political climate changed: The voters rejected the previously popular governor.

Always use lowercase for a list or an appositive that follows a colon.

> Students were divided into two groups: residents and commuters.

37g Abbreviations

Capitalize abbreviations for departments and agencies of government, organizations, and corporations, as well as the call letters of radio and television stations: *EPA, FBI, DKNY, IBM, WERS, KNBC-TV.*

38 Abbreviations

In the text of a paper, use abbreviations only when they are clearly appropriate and universally understood (such as *Dr., mm, IQ*).

38a Before and after a name

Use standard abbreviations for titles immediately before and after proper names.

TITLES BEFORE PROPER NAMES	TITLES AFTER PROPER NAMES
Ms. Nancy Linehan	Thomas Hines Jr.
Mr. Raphael Zabala	Anita Lor, PhD
Dr. Margaret Simmons	Robert Simkowski, MD
Rev. John Stone	Mia Chin, LLD

Do not abbreviate a title if it is not used with a proper name: *My criminology professor* [not *prof.*] *was an expert in constitutional law.*

38b Organizations, companies, countries

Familiar abbreviations for names of organizations, companies, and countries are generally acceptable: *CIA, FBI, NAACP, EPA, YMCA, NBC, USA.*

If you have any doubt about whether your readers will understand an abbreviation or whether the abbreviation is potentially unfamiliar or ambiguous, write the full name followed immediately by the abbreviation in parentheses the first time you mention it. Then use just the abbreviation in the rest of the paper. *AMA*, for instance, could refer to the American Medical Association or the American Management Association.

38c Units of measurement and time

Use abbreviations for units of measurement and of time that are preceded by a number. Spell out units if they are used alone.

> 5 cm
>
> 20 µA
>
> 10-km race
>
> 10:00 p.m.
>
> Doses were specified in milliliters.
>
> Results were measured in seconds.

The following are typical abbreviations for units of measurement. While most social science and related fields use metric measures, you may have occasion to use U.S. standard units in some of your work.

m, cm, mm	km, kph	g, kg, mg, µg	L, mL, dL
dB	ppm	Hz, kHz	W, kW
°C, °F	A, µA	hr, min	s, ms, ns
lb	yd, ft, in.	mi, mph	

Do not use periods after abbreviations for units of measurement or time (except the abbreviations *in.* for inch and *a.m.* and *p.m.*).

Do not abbreviate *day*, *week*, *month*, or *year*, even when preceded by a number.

38d Latin abbreviations

Although Latin abbreviations are appropriate in footnotes and reference lists, use the appropriate English phrases in the text of a paper.

> cf. (*confer*, "compare")
>
> e.g. (*exempli gratia*, "for example")
>
> etc. (*et cetera*, "and so forth")
>
> i.e. (*id est*, "that is")
>
> N.B. (*nota bene*, "note well")

One exception is the abbreviation et al. (*et alii*, "and others"). Using this abbreviation in the text of a paper is acceptable only if the source has six or more authors, or in the second and subsequent in-text citations of any source. The first time you cite a source with fewer than six authors in the text, always include the last names of all authors.

38e Plural of abbreviations

For the plural of most abbreviations, add -*s* (do not use an apostrophe): *PhDs*, *RTs*, *EMTs*.

Do not add -*s* to indicate the plural of units of measurement.

mm (*not* mms)

L (*not* Ls)

in. (*not* ins.)

38f Other uses of abbreviations

Other commonly accepted abbreviations and symbols include *BC*, *AD*, *No.*, and *$*. The abbreviation *BC* ("before Christ") follows a date, and *AD* ("*anno Domini*") precedes a date. Acceptable alternatives are *BCE* ("before the common era") and *CE* ("common era"). Both follow a date.

40 BC (or 40 BCE)	No. 12 (or no. 12)
AD 44 (or 44 CE)	$150

Avoid using *No.* or *$* unless it is accompanied by a specific number.

38g Inappropriate abbreviations

Abbreviations for the following are not commonly accepted in the text of a paper.

DAYS OF THE WEEK Monday (*not* Mon.)

HOLIDAYS Christmas (*not* Xmas)

MONTHS January, February (*not* Jan., Feb.)

COURSES OF STUDY political science (*not* poli. sci.)

DIVISIONS OF WRITTEN WORKS chapter, page (*not* ch., p.)

STATES AND COUNTRIES Florida (*not* FL or Fla.)

PARTS OF A BUSINESS NAME   Adams Lighting Company
(*not* Adams Lighting Co.)

NOTE: For use of abbreviations in documenting sources,
see sections 13 and 14.

39   Numbers

In a paper, you may need to communicate statistics,
survey results, or other data. In some cases, you will use
numerals (*15*, for instance); in others, you will spell out
the numbers (*eight*).

39a   Using numerals

Use numerals to represent all numbers 10 and above
and for all numbers that precede a unit of measurement. (See 39b for exceptions.)

> 12 mm, 4 cm
>
> 5-ft gap

Use numerals for all numbers in the abstract of a paper.
The following are other acceptable uses of numerals.

DATES   July 4, 1776; 56 BC; AD 30

ADDRESSES   77 Latches Lane, 519 West 42nd Street

PERCENTAGES   5%

FRACTIONS, DECIMALS   ½, 0.047

SCORES   7 to 3, 21–18

AGES   5-year-old, average age 37

SURVEYS   4 out of 5

EXACT AMOUNTS OF MONEY $105.37, $0.05

DIVISIONS OF BOOKS   volume 3, chapter 4, page 189

DIVISIONS OF PLAYS   act 3, scene 3

TIME OF DAY   4:00 p.m., 1:30 a.m.

ORDINALS ABOVE 10   12th

39b   Using words for numbers

Spell out the numbers one through nine (unless they
are used in the ways noted in 39a).

Spell out numbers for universally accepted uses or titles: *The Ten Commandments, The Three Stooges.*

A number at the beginning of a sentence should be spelled out, but it is preferable to reword the sentence to avoid the number at the beginning.

NOTE: Numerals and spelled-out numbers may appear together in the same sentence or paragraph. Use the rules in 39a and 39b to determine whether each number should be spelled out or expressed as a numeral.

Of 35 students taking the test, only three finished in the allotted time.

40 Italics

This section describes conventional uses for italics.

40a Titles of works

Titles of the following types of works are italicized.

TITLES OF BOOKS   *The Invisible Line, Governing Through Crime, Freakonomics*

JOURNALS AND MAGAZINES   *Psychological Review, Journal of Social Work, American Journal of Political Science*

NEWSPAPERS   the *Baltimore Sun,* the *Wall Street Journal*

PAMPHLETS   *Common Sense, Facts About Marijuana*

PLAYS   *King Lear, Wicked*

FILMS   *A Beautiful Mind, An Inconvenient Truth*

TELEVISION PROGRAMS   *The Voice, Frontline*

RADIO PROGRAMS   *All Things Considered*

MUSICAL COMPOSITIONS   *Porgy and Bess*

WORKS OF VISUAL ART   *American Gothic*

COMIC STRIPS   *Dilbert*

WEBSITES   *ZDNet, Google*

VIDEO GAMES   *Dragon Age, Call of Duty*

Titles of other works, such as journal or newspaper articles, short stories, essays, and songs, are enclosed in quotation marks in the text of a paper. (See also 35b.)

For guidelines on formatting titles in the reference list, see 11b.

NOTE: Do not use italics when referring to the Bible; titles of books in the Bible (Genesis, not *Genesis*); the titles of legal documents (the Constitution, not the *Constitution*); or the titles of your own papers.

40b Words as words and other uses

Italicize words and letters used in the following ways.

WORDS AS WORDS   The 3-year-old could pronounce *know* but not *snow*.

LETTERS AS LETTERS   Many children with dyslexia cannot distinguish *b* from *d*.

VARIABLES AND STATISTICAL NOTATION $F(1, 14)$, $p = .04$

GENERA, SPECIES, VARIETIES   *Alligator sinensis*

FIRST USE OF KEY TERM   The process is called *photosynthesis*.

40c Ships, aircraft, spacecraft

Italicize names of specific ships, aircraft, and spacecraft.

> *Arbella, Spirit of St. Louis, Challenger*

40d Foreign words

Italicize foreign words used in an English sentence.

> *Gemeinschaften* are communities in which members are strongly attached to the values and beliefs of the group.

EXCEPTION: Do not italicize foreign words that have become part of the English language.

laissez-faire   per diem
fait accompli   modus operandi
et al.   per se

41   Spelling

A spell checker is a useful tool, but be aware of its limitations. A spell checker won't catch words commonly confused (*accept, except*) or common typographical errors (*own* for *won*). You still need to proofread, and you may need to turn to the dictionary or to the glossary of usage at the back of this book.

41a Major spelling rules

If you need to improve your spelling, review the following rules and exceptions.

i before e   In general, use *i* before *e* except after *c* and except when sounded like "ay," as in *neighbor* and *weigh*.

I BEFORE E	relieve, believe, sieve, niece, fierce, frieze
E BEFORE I	receive, deceive, sleigh, freight, eight
EXCEPTIONS	seize, either, weird, height, foreign, leisure

Adding suffixes   Generally, drop a final silent *-e* when adding a suffix that begins with a vowel. Keep the final *-e* if the suffix begins with a consonant.

| desire, desiring | achieve, achievement |
| remove, removable | care, careful |

Words such as *changeable, judgment, argument,* and *truly* are exceptions.

   If a final consonant is preceded by a single vowel and the consonant ends a one-syllable word or a stressed syllable, double the consonant when adding a suffix beginning with a vowel.

| bet, betting | occur, occurrence |
| commit, committed | |

Adding -s and -ed   When adding *-s* or *-ed* to words ending in *-y*, ordinarily change *-y* to *-ie* when the *-y* is preceded by a consonant. Add just an *-s* or add *-ed* when *-y* is preceded by a vowel.

| comedy, comedies | monkey, monkeys |
| dry, dried | play, played |

With proper names ending in *-y*, however, do not change the *-y* to *-i* even if it is preceded by a consonant: *the Dougherty family, the Doughertys.*

Plurals   Add *-s* to form the plural of most nouns; add *-es* to singular nouns ending in *-s, -sh, -ch,* and *-x*.

| table, tables | church, churches |
| paper, papers | dish, dishes |

Ordinarily add -*s* to nouns ending in -*o* when the -*o* is preceded by a vowel. Add -*es* when the -*o* is preceded by a consonant.

radio, radios	hero, heroes
video, videos	tomato, tomatoes

To form the plural of a hyphenated compound word, add the -*s* to the chief word even if it does not appear at the end.

mother-in-law, mothers-in-law

NOTE: English words derived from other languages such as Latin, Greek, or French sometimes form the plural as they would in their original language.

medium, media	chateau, chateaux
criterion, criteria	

41b Spelling variations

Following is a list of some common words spelled differently in American and British English. Consult a dictionary for others.

AMERICAN	BRITISH
canceled, traveled	cancelled, travelled
color, humor	colour, humour
judgment	judgement
check	cheque
realize, apologize	realise, apologise
defense	defence
anemia, anesthetic	anaemia, anaesthetic
theater, center	theatre, centre
fetus	foetus
mold, smolder	mould, smoulder
civilization	civilisation
connection, inflection	connexion, inflexion

42 Hyphenation

In addition to the following guidelines, a dictionary can provide help with hyphenation.

42a Compound words

The dictionary will tell you whether to treat a compound word as a hyphenated compound (*water-repellent*), as one word (*waterproof*), or as two words (*water table*). If the compound word is not in the dictionary, treat it as two words.

> The prosecutor did not cross-examine any witnesses.

> The research committee considered the pros and cons of a crossover trial.

> The sample represented a cross section of voters in the third district.

42b Words functioning together as an adjective

When two or more words function together as an adjective before a noun, connect them with a hyphen. Generally, do not use a hyphen when such compounds follow the noun.

> well-known candidate, candidate who is well known
>
> stress-inducing activity
>
> middle-school students
>
> low-impact agriculture
>
> 10th-grade assignments, sixth-grade teacher
>
> 1-mm tolerance
>
> three-fifths representation

Do not use a hyphen after an adverb ending in *-ly*, in a compound that includes a comparative or superlative, with chemical compounds, with foreign phrases, or with a compound ending in a number.

> rapidly growing bacteria
>
> longest running experiment
>
> sodium hydroxide production
>
> a priori condition
>
> Type 2 diabetes

NOTE: In a series of hyphenated adjectives modifying the same noun, hyphens are suspended: *The test was administered to all second-, third-, and fourth-year students.*

42c Suffixes and prefixes

Most suffixes and prefixes do not require a hyphen.

PREFIXES	SUFFIXES
*anti*war	human*like*
*inter*scholastic	search*able*
*non*consenting	
*semi*circle	
*un*sustainable	

There are some exceptions. Hyphens are used with the prefixes *all-*, *ex-*, and *self-* and the suffix *-elect*; with prefixes before capitalized words or numbers; with prefixes of more than two words; and with terms that would otherwise be confusing.

all-encompassing	un-American
ex-president	non-stress-inducing
self-effacing	re-create (create again)
senator-elect	re-sent (sent again)

A hyphen is usually used to avoid a double vowel, but most *pre-* and *re-* words and some other words that are well established do not use the hyphen in such a case.

anti-inflammatory	reenter
anti-intellectual	reemerge
co-opt	preexisting
co-owner	cooperate
intra-arterial	microorganism

42d Hyphenation at ends of lines

Only words that already contain a hyphen may break at the end of a line of text. If your writing software automatically breaks words at the ends of lines, disable that setting.

Email addresses, URLs, and other electronic addresses need special attention when they occur at the end of a line of text. Do not insert a hyphen to divide electronic addresses. Instead, break an email address after the @ symbol or before a period. Break a URL after a double slash or before any other mark of punctuation.

Glossaries

Glossary of usage

This glossary includes words commonly confused, words commonly misused, and words that are nonstandard. It also lists colloquialisms that may be appropriate in informal speech but are inappropriate in formal writing.

a, an Use *an* before a vowel sound, *a* before a consonant sound: *an apple, a peach*. Problems sometimes arise with words beginning with *h* or *u*. If the *h* is silent, the word begins with a vowel sound, so use *an: an hour, an heir, an honest senator*. If the *h* is pronounced, the word begins with a consonant sound, so use *a: a hospital, a historian, a hotel*. Words such as *university* and *union* begin with a consonant sound, so use *a: a union*. Words such as *uncle* and *umbrella* begin with a vowel sound, so use *an: an umbrella*. When an abbreviation or acronym begins with a vowel sound, use *an: an EKG, an MRI*.

accept, except *Accept* is a verb meaning "to receive." *Except* is usually a preposition meaning "excluding." *I will accept all the packages except that one. Except* is also a verb meaning "to exclude." *Please except that item from the list.*

adapt, adopt *Adapt* means "to adjust or become accustomed"; it is usually followed by *to. Adopt* means "to take as one's own." *Our family adopted a Vietnamese child, who quickly adapted to his new life.*

adverse, averse *Adverse* means "unfavorable." *Averse* means "opposed" or "reluctant"; it is usually followed by *to. I am averse to your proposal because it could have an adverse impact on the economy.*

advice, advise *Advice* is a noun, *advise* a verb. *We advise you to follow John's advice.*

affect, effect *Affect* is usually a verb meaning "to influence." *Effect* is usually a noun meaning "result." *The drug did not affect the disease, and it had adverse side effects. Effect* can also be a verb meaning "to bring about." *Only the president can effect such a change.*

all ready, already *All ready* means "completely prepared." *Already* means "previously." *Susan was all ready for the concert, but her friends had already left.*

all right *All right*, written as two words, is correct. *Alright* is nonstandard.

all together, altogether *All together* means "everyone gathered." *Altogether* means "entirely." *We were not altogether sure that we could bring the family all together for the reunion.*

allusion, illusion An *allusion* is an indirect reference; an *illusion* is a misconception or false impression. *Did you* *catch my allusion to Shakespeare? Mirrors give the room an illusion of depth.*

a lot   *A lot* is two words. Do not write *alot*.

among, between   Ordinarily, use *among* with three or more entities, *between* with two. *The prize was divided among several contestants. You have a choice between carrots and beans.*

amoral, immoral   *Amoral* means "neither moral nor immoral"; it also means "not caring about moral judgments." *Immoral* means "morally wrong." *Many business courses are taught from an amoral perspective. Murder is immoral.*

amount, number   Use *amount* with quantities that cannot be counted; use *number* with those that can. *This recipe calls for a large amount of sugar. We have a large number of toads in our garden.*

an   See *a, an.*

and/or   Avoid *and/or* except in technical or legal documents.

anxious   *Anxious* means "worried" or "apprehensive." In formal writing, avoid using *anxious* to mean "eager." *We are eager (not anxious) to see your new house.*

anybody, anyone   See pages 159 and 169.

anyone, any one   *Anyone*, an indefinite pronoun, means "any person at all." *Any one* refers to a particular person or thing in a group. *Anyone in the class may choose any one of the books to read.*

anyways, anywheres   *Anyways* and *anywheres* are nonstandard for *anyway* and *anywhere.*

as   *As* is sometimes used to mean "because." But do not use it if there is any chance of ambiguity. *We canceled the picnic because (not as) it began raining. As* here could mean "because" or "when."

as, like   See *like, as.*

averse   See *adverse, averse.*

awhile, a while   *Awhile* is an adverb; it can modify a verb, but it cannot be the object of a preposition such as *for.* The two-word form *a while* is a noun preceded by an article and therefore can be the object of a preposition. *Stay awhile. Stay for a while.*

back up, backup   *Back up* is a verb phrase. *Back up the car carefully. Be sure to back up your hard drive. Backup* is a noun often meaning "duplicate of electronically stored data." *Keep your backup in a safe place. Backup* can also be used as an adjective. *I regularly create backup disks.*

bad, badly   *Bad* is an adjective, *badly* an adverb. *They felt bad about being early and ruining the surprise. Her arm hurt badly after she slid into second.* See section 28.

being as, being that   *Being as* and *being that* are nonstandard expressions. Write *because* instead.

beside, besides   *Beside* is a preposition meaning "at the side of" or "next to." *Annie sleeps with a flashlight beside her bed. Besides* is a preposition meaning "except" or "in addition to." *No one besides Terrie can have that ice cream. Besides* is also an adverb meaning "in addition." *I'm not hungry; besides, I don't like ice cream.*

between   See *among, between.*

bring, take   Use *bring* when an object is being transported toward you, *take* when it is being moved away. *Please bring me a glass of water. Please take these magazines to Mr. Scott.*

can, may   *Can* is traditionally reserved for ability, *may* for permission. *Can you speak French? May I help you?*

capital, capitol   *Capital* refers to a city, *capitol* to a building where lawmakers meet. *The residents of the state capital protested the development plans. The capitol has undergone extensive renovations. Capital* also refers to wealth or resources.

censor, censure   *Censor* means "to remove or suppress material considered objectionable." *Censure* means "to criticize severely." *The school's policy of censoring books has been censured by the media.*

cite, site   *Cite* means "to quote as an authority or example." *Site* is usually a noun meaning "a particular place." *He cited the zoning law in his argument against the proposed site of the gas station.* Locations on the Internet are usually referred to as *sites.*

complement, compliment   *Complement* is a verb meaning "to go with or complete" or a noun meaning "something that completes." As a verb, *compliment* means "to flatter"; as a noun, it means "flattering remark." *Her skill at rushing the net complements his skill at volleying. Sheiying's music arrangements receive many compliments.*

conscience, conscious   *Conscience* is a noun meaning "moral principles"; *conscious* is an adjective meaning "aware or alert." *Let your conscience be your guide. Were you conscious of his love for you?*

continual, continuous   *Continual* means "repeated regularly and frequently." *She grew weary of the continual telephone calls. Continuous* means "extended or prolonged without interruption." *The broken siren made a continuous wail.*

could care less   Write *couldn't care less* when referring to someone who does not care about something. (*Could care less* is nonstandard and means that the person described does care.)

could of   *Could of* is nonstandard for *could have.*

council, counsel   A *council* is a deliberative body, and a *councilor* is a member of such a body. *Counsel* usually means "advice" and can also mean "lawyer"; a *counselor* is one who gives advice or guidance. *The councilors met to draft the council's position paper. The pastor offered wise counsel to the troubled teenager.*

criteria   *Criteria* is the plural of *criterion*, which means "a standard, rule, or test on which a judgment or decision can be based." *The only criterion for the scholarship is ability.*

data   *Data* is a plural noun meaning "facts or results." *The new data suggest that our theory is correct.* Except in scientific writing, *data* is increasingly being accepted as a singular noun.

different from, different than   Ordinarily, write *different from. Your sense of style is different from Jim's.* However, *different than* is acceptable to avoid an awkward construction. *Please let me know if your plans are different than* (to avoid *from what*) *they were six weeks ago.*

disinterested, uninterested   *Disinterested* means "impartial, objective"; *uninterested* means "not interested." *We sought the advice of a disinterested counselor to help us solve our problem. Mark was uninterested in anyone's opinion but his own.*

each   See pages 159 and 169.

effect   See *affect, effect.*

either   See pages 159 and 169.

elicit, illicit   *Elicit* is a verb meaning "to bring out" or "to evoke." *Illicit* is an adjective meaning "unlawful." *The reporter was unable to elicit any information from the police about illicit drug traffic.*

emigrate from, immigrate to   *Emigrate* means "to leave one place to settle in another." *My great-grandfather emigrated from Russia to escape the religious pogroms. Immigrate* means "to enter another place and reside there." *Thousands of Bosnians immigrated to the United States in the 1990s.*

etc.   Avoid ending a list with *etc.* It is more emphatic to end with an example, and usually readers will understand that the list is not exhaustive. When you don't wish to end with an example, *and so on* is more graceful than *etc.*

everybody, everyone   See pages 159 and 169.

everyone, every one   *Everyone* is an indefinite pronoun.
Everyone wanted to go. Every one, the pronoun *one* preceded
by the adjective *every*, means "each individual or thing
in a particular group." *Every one* is usually followed by *of*.
Every one of the missing books was found.

except   See *accept, except*.

farther, further   *Farther* describes distances. *Further*
suggests quantity or degree. *Detroit is farther from Miami
than I thought. You extended the curfew further than
necessary.*

fewer, less   *Fewer* refers to items that can be counted;
less refers to items that cannot be counted. *Fewer people
are living in the city. Please put less sugar in my tea.*

firstly   *Firstly* sounds pretentious, and it leads to the
ungainly series *firstly, secondly, thirdly, fourthly*, and so on.
Write *first, second, third, fourth* instead.

further   See *farther, further*.

good, well   See page 177.

hanged, hung   *Hanged* is the past-tense and past-
participle form of the verb *hang*, meaning "to execute."
The prisoner was hanged at dawn. Hung is the past-tense
and past-participle form of the verb *hang*, meaning
"to fasten or suspend." *The stockings were hung by the
chimney with care.*

hardly   Avoid expressions such as *can't hardly* and *not
hardly*, which are considered double negatives. *I can* (not
can't) *hardly describe my elation at getting the job.*

hopefully   *Hopefully* means "in a hopeful manner." *We
looked hopefully to the future.* Some usage experts object
to the use of *hopefully* as a sentence adverb, apparently
on grounds of clarity. To be safe, avoid using *hopefully* in
sentences such as the following: *Hopefully, your son will
recover soon.* Instead, indicate who is doing the hoping:
I hope that your son will recover soon.

however   Some writers object to *however* at the
beginning of a sentence, but experts advise placing the
word according to the meaning and emphasis intended.
Any of the following sentences is correct, depending on
the intended contrast. *Pam decided, however, to attend the
lecture. However, Pam decided to attend the lecture.* (She had
been considering other activities.) *Pam, however, decided
to attend the lecture.* (Unlike someone else, Pam opted for
the lecture.)

hung   See *hanged, hung*.

illusion   See *allusion, illusion*.

immigrate   See *emigrate from, immigrate to.*

immoral   See *amoral, immoral.*

imply, infer   *Imply* means "to suggest or state indirectly"; *infer* means "to draw a conclusion." *John implied that he knew all about computers, but the interviewer inferred that John was inexperienced.*

in, into   *In* indicates location or condition; *into* indicates movement or a change in condition. *They found the lost letters in a box after moving into the house.*

irregardless   *Irregardless* is nonstandard. Use *regardless.*

is when, is where   See section 21c.

its, it's   *Its* is a possessive pronoun; *it's* is a contraction for *it is. It's always fun to watch a dog chase its tail.*

kind of, sort of   Avoid using *kind of* or *sort of* to mean "somewhat." *The movie was a little* (not *kind of*) *boring.* Do not put *a* after either phrase. *That kind of* (not *kind of a*) *salesclerk annoys me.*

lay, lie   See page 163.

lead, led   *Lead* is a metallic element; it is a noun. *Led* is the past tense of the verb *lead. He led me to the treasure.*

less   See *fewer, less.*

liable   *Liable* means "obligated" or "responsible." Do not use it to mean "likely." *You're likely* (not *liable*) *to trip if you don't tie your shoelaces.*

lie, lay   See page 163.

like, as   *Like* is a preposition, not a subordinating conjunction. It should be followed only by a noun or a noun phrase. *As* is a subordinating conjunction that introduces a subordinate clause. In casual speech, you may say *She looks like she has not slept.* But in formal writing, use *as. She looks as if she has not slept.*

loose, lose   *Loose* is an adjective meaning "not securely fastened." *Lose* is a verb meaning "to misplace" or "to not win." *Did you lose all your loose change?*

may   See *can, may.*

maybe, may be   *Maybe* is an adverb meaning "possibly"; *may be* is a verb phrase. *Maybe the sun will shine tomorrow. Tomorrow may be a brighter day.*

may of, might of   *May of* and *might of* are nonstandard for *may have* and *might have.*

media, medium   *Media* is the plural of *medium. Of all the media that cover the Olympics, television is the medium that best captures the spectacle of the events.*

must of   *Must of* is nonstandard for *must have.*

myself   *Myself* is a reflexive or intensive pronoun. Reflexive: *I cut myself.* Intensive: *I will drive you myself.* Do not use *myself* in place of *I* or *me*: *He gave the plants to Melinda and me* (not *myself*).

neither   See pages 159 and 169.

none   See page 159.

nowheres   *Nowheres* is nonstandard for *nowhere.*

number   See *amount, number.*

off of   *Off* is sufficient. Omit *of.*

passed, past   *Passed* is the past tense of the verb *pass. Emily passed me a slice of cake. Past* usually means "belonging to a former time" or "beyond a time or place." *Our past president spoke until past 10:00. The hotel is just past the station.*

plus   *Plus* should not be used to join independent clauses. *This raincoat is dirty; moreover* (not *plus*), *it has a hole in it.*

precede, proceed   *Precede* means "to come before." *Proceed* means "to go forward." *As we proceeded up the mountain, we saw evidence that some hikers had preceded us.*

principal, principle   *Principal* is a noun meaning "the head of a school or an organization" or "a sum of money." It is also an adjective meaning "most important." *Principle* is a noun meaning "a basic truth or law." *The principal expelled her for three principal reasons. We believe in the principle of equal justice for all.*

proceed, precede   See *precede, proceed.*

quote, quotation   *Quote* is a verb; *quotation* is a noun. Avoid using *quote* as a shortened form of *quotation. Her quotations* (not *quotes*) *from Shakespeare intrigued us.*

real, really   *Real* is an adjective; *really* is an adverb. *Real* is sometimes used informally as an adverb, but avoid this use in formal writing. *She was really* (not *real*) *angry.* See also section 28.

reason . . . is because   See section 21c.

reason why   The expression *reason why* is redundant. *The reason* (not *The reason why*) *Jones lost the election is clear.*

respectfully, respectively   *Respectfully* means "showing or marked by respect." *He respectfully submitted his opinion. Respectively* means "each in the order given." *John, Tom, and Larry were a butcher, a baker, and a lawyer, respectively.*

sensual, sensuous   *Sensual* means "gratifying the physical senses," especially those associated with sexual pleasure. *Sensuous* means "pleasing to the senses," especially involving art, music, and nature. *The sensuous music and balmy air led the dancers to more sensual movements.*

set, sit   *Set* means "to put" or "to place"; *sit* means "to be seated." *She set the dough in a warm corner of the kitchen. The cat sits in the warmest part of the room.*

should of   *Should of* is nonstandard for *should have*.

since   Do not use *since* to mean "because" if there is any chance of ambiguity. *Because* (not *Since*) *we won the game, we have been celebrating. Since* here could mean "because" or "from the time that."

sit   See *set, sit*.

site, cite   See *cite, site*.

somebody, someone, something   See pages 159 and 169.

suppose to   Write *supposed to*.

sure and   *Sure and* is nonstandard for *sure to*. *Be sure to* (not *sure and*) *bring a gift for the host.*

take   See *bring, take*.

than, then   *Than* is a conjunction used in comparisons; *then* is an adverb denoting time. *That pizza is more than I can eat. Tom laughed, and then we recognized him.*

that   See *who, which, that*.

that, which   Many writers reserve *that* for restrictive clauses, *which* for nonrestrictive clauses. (See p. 196.)

then   See *than, then*.

there, their, they're   *There* is an adverb specifying place; it is also an expletive (placeholder). Adverb: *Sylvia is sitting there patiently.* Expletive: *There are two plums left.* (See also p. 241.) *Their* is a possessive pronoun. *Fred and Jane finally washed their car. They're* is a contraction of *they are*. *They're late today.*

to, too, two   *To* is a preposition; *too* is an adverb; *two* is a number. *Too many of your shots slice to the left, but the last two were right on the mark.*

toward, towards   *Toward* and *towards* are generally interchangeable, although *toward* is preferred in American English.

try and   *Try and* is nonstandard for *try to*. *I will try to* (not *try and*) *be better about writing to you.*

uninterested   See *disinterested, uninterested*.

unique   See page 178.

use to Write *used to*. *We used to live in an apartment.*

utilize *Utilize* is often a pretentious substitute for *use*; in most cases, *use* is sufficient. *I used* (not *utilized*) *the printer.*

wait for, wait on *Wait for* means "to be in readiness for" or "to await." *Wait on* means "to serve." *We're waiting for* (not *waiting on*) *Ruth before we can leave.*

ways *Ways* is colloquial when used in place of *way* to mean "distance." *The city is a long way* (not *ways*) *from here.*

weather, whether The noun *weather* refers to the state of the atmosphere. *Whether* is a conjunction indicating a choice between alternatives. *We wondered whether the weather would clear up in time for our picnic.*

well, good See page 177.

which See *that, which* and *who, which, that*.

while Avoid using *while* to mean "although" or "whereas" if there is any chance of ambiguity. *Although* (not *While*) *Gloria lost money in the slot machine, Tom won it at roulette.* Here *While* could mean either "although" or "at the same time that."

who, which, that Use *who*, not *which*, to refer to persons. Generally, use *that* to refer to things or, occasionally, to a group or class of people. *The player who* (not *that* or *which*) *made the basket at the buzzer was named MVP. The team that scores the most points in this game will win the tournament.*

who, whom See section 27d.

who's, whose *Who's* is a contraction of *who is; whose* is a possessive pronoun. *Who's ready for more popcorn? Whose coat is this?*

would of *Would of* is nonstandard for *would have*.

you See page 172.

your, you're *Your* is a possessive pronoun; *you're* is a contraction of *you are*. *Is that your bike? You're in the finals.*

Glossary of grammatical terms

This glossary gives definitions for parts of speech, such as nouns; parts of sentences, such as subjects; and types of sentences, clauses, and phrases.

If you are looking up the name of an error (sentence fragment, for example), consult the index or the table of contents instead.

absolute phrase   A word group that modifies a whole clause or sentence, usually consisting of a noun followed by a participle or participial phrase: *Her words echoing in the large arena,* the senator mesmerized the crowd.

active vs. passive voice   When a verb is in the active voice, the subject of the sentence does the action: *Hernando caught* the ball. In the passive voice, the subject receives the action: The *ball was caught* by Hernando. Often the actor does not appear in a passive-voice sentence: The *ball was caught.* See also section 17.

adjective   A word used to modify (describe) a noun or pronoun: the *frisky* horse, *rare old* stamps, *16* candles, the *blue* one. Adjectives usually answer one of these questions: Which one? What kind of? How many or how much? See also section 28.

adjective clause   A subordinate clause that modifies a noun or pronoun. An adjective clause begins with a relative pronoun (*who, whom, whose, which, that*) or with a relative adverb (*when, where*) and usually appears right after the word it modifies: The book *that goes unread* is a writer's worst nightmare. See also *subordinate clause.*

adverb   A word used to modify a verb, an adjective, or another adverb: rides *smoothly, unusually* attractive, *very* slowly. An adverb usually answers one of these questions: When? Where? How? Why? Under what conditions? How often? To what degree? See also section 28.

adverb clause   A subordinate clause that modifies a verb (or occasionally an adjective or adverb). An adverb clause begins with a subordinating conjunction such as *although, because, if, unless,* or *when* and usually appears at the beginning or end of a sentence: *When the sun went down,* the hikers prepared their camp. See also *subordinate clause; subordinating conjunction.*

agreement   See sections 25 and 27.

antecedent   A noun or pronoun to which a pronoun refers: When the *battery* wears down, we recharge *it.* The noun *battery* is the antecedent of the pronoun *it.*

appositive A noun or noun phrase that renames a nearby noun or pronoun: Bloggers, *conversationalists at heart*, are the online equivalent of talk show hosts.

article The word *a*, *an*, or *the*, used to mark a noun. See also section 31b.

case See sections 27c and 27d.

clause A word group containing a subject, a verb, and any objects, complements, or modifiers. See *independent clause*; *subordinate clause*.

collective noun See sections 25e and 27a.

common noun See section 37a.

complement See *object complement*; *subject complement*.

complex sentence A sentence consisting of one independent clause and one or more subordinate clauses. In the following example, the subordinate clause is italicized: We walked along the river *until we came to the bridge*.

compound-complex sentence A sentence consisting of at least two independent clauses and at least one subordinate clause: Jan dictated a story, and the children wrote whatever he said. In the preceding sentence, the subordinate clause is *whatever he said*. The two independent clauses are *Jan dictated a story* and *the children wrote whatever he said*.

compound sentence A sentence consisting of two or more independent clauses, with no subordinate clauses. The clauses are usually joined with a comma and a coordinating conjunction (*and, but, or, nor, for, so, yet*) or with a semicolon: The car broke down, *but* a rescue van arrived within minutes. A shark was spotted near shore; people left the water immediately.

conjunction A joining word. See *conjunctive adverb*; *coordinating conjunction*; *correlative conjunction*; *subordinating conjunction*.

conjunctive adverb An adverb used with a semicolon to connect independent clauses: The bus was stuck in traffic; *therefore*, the team was late for the game. The most commonly used conjunctive adverbs are *consequently*, *furthermore*, *however*, *moreover*, *nevertheless*, *then*, *therefore*, and *thus*. See page 201 for a longer list.

coordinating conjunction One of the following words, used to join elements of equal grammatical rank: *and*, *but*, *or*, *nor*, *for*, *so*, *yet*.

correlative conjunction A pair of conjunctions connecting grammatically equal elements: *either . . . or*, *neither . . . nor*, *whether . . . or*, *not only . . . but also*, *both . . . and*. See also section 18b.

count noun   See page 187.

demonstrative pronoun   A pronoun used to identify or point to a noun: *this, that, these, those. This* is my favorite chair.

direct object   A word or word group that receives the action of the verb: The hungry cat clawed *the bag of dry food.* The complete direct object is *the bag of dry food.* The simple direct object is always a noun or a pronoun, in this case *bag.*

expletive   The word *there* or *it* when used at the beginning of a sentence to delay the subject: *There* are eight planes waiting to take off. *It* is healthy to eat breakfast every day. The delayed subjects are the noun *planes* and the infinitive phrase *to eat breakfast every day.*

gerund   A verb form ending in *-ing* used as a noun: *Reading* aloud helps children appreciate language. The gerund *reading* is used as the subject of the verb *helps.*

gerund phrase   A gerund and its objects, complements, or modifiers. A gerund phrase always functions as a noun, usually as a subject, a subject complement, a direct object, or the object of a preposition. In the following example, the phrase functions as a direct object: We tried *planting tulips.*

helping verb   One of the following words, when used with a main verb: *be, am, is, are, was, were, being, been; has, have, had; do, does, did; can, will, shall, should, could, would, may, might, must.* Helping verbs always precede main verbs: *will work, is working, had worked.* See also *modal verb.*

indefinite pronoun   A pronoun that refers to a nonspecific person or thing: *Something* is burning. The most common indefinite pronouns are *all, another, any, anybody, anyone, anything, both, each, either, everybody, everyone, everything, few, many, neither, nobody, none, no one, nothing, one, some, somebody, someone,* and *something.* See also pages 159 and 169.

independent clause   A word group containing a subject and a verb that could or does stand alone as a sentence. In addition to at least one independent clause, many sentences contain subordinate clauses that function as adjectives, adverbs, or nouns. See also *clause; subordinate clause.*

indirect object   A noun or pronoun that names to whom or for whom the action of a sentence is done: We gave *her* some leftover yarn. An indirect object always precedes a direct object, in this case *some leftover yarn.*

infinitive   The word *to* followed by the base form of a verb: *to think, to dream*.

infinitive phrase   An infinitive and its objects, complements, or modifiers. An infinitive phrase can function as a noun, an adjective, or an adverb. Noun: *To live without health insurance* is risky. Adjective: The Nineteenth Amendment gave women the right *to vote*. Adverb: Volunteers knocked on doors *to rescue people from the flood*.

intensive or reflexive pronoun   A pronoun ending in *-self* (or *-selves*): *myself, yourself, himself, herself, itself, ourselves, yourselves, themselves*. An intensive pronoun emphasizes a noun or another pronoun: I *myself* don't have a job. A reflexive pronoun names a receiver of an action identical with the doer of the action: Did Paula cut *herself*?

interjection   A word expressing surprise or emotion: *Oh! Wow! Hey! Hooray!*

interrogative pronoun   A pronoun used to introduce a question: *who, whom, whose, which, what. What* does history teach us?

intransitive verb   See *transitive and intransitive verbs*.

irregular verb   See *regular and irregular verbs*. See also section 26a.

linking verb   A verb that links a subject to a subject complement, a word or word group that renames or describes the subject: The winner *was* a teacher. The cherries *taste* sour. The most common linking verbs are forms of *be: be, am, is, are, was, were, being, been*. The following sometimes function as linking verbs: *appear, become, feel, grow, look, make, seem, smell, sound, taste*. See also *subject complement*.

modal verb   A helping verb that cannot be used as a main verb. There are nine modals: *can, could, may, might, must, shall, should, will*, and *would*. We *must* shut the windows before the storm. The verb phrase *ought to* is often classified as a modal as well. See also *helping verb*.

modifier   A word, phrase, or clause that describes or qualifies the meaning of a word. Modifiers include adjectives, adverbs, prepositional phrases, participial phrases, some infinitive phrases, and adjective and adverb clauses.

mood   See section 26c.

noncount noun   See pages 187–188.

noun   The name of a person, place, thing, or concept (*freedom*, for example): The *lion* in the *cage* growled at the *zookeeper*.

noun clause   A subordinate clause that functions like a noun, usually as a subject, a subject complement, a direct object, or the object of a preposition. In the following sentence, the italicized noun clause functions as the subject: *Whoever leaves the house last* must lock the door. Noun clauses usually begin with *how, who, whom, whoever, that, what, whatever, whether,* or *why.*

noun equivalent   A word or word group that functions like a noun: a pronoun, a noun and its modifiers, a gerund phrase, some infinitive phrases, or a noun clause.

object   See *direct object; indirect object.*

object complement   A word or word group that renames or describes a direct object. It always appears after the direct object: The kiln makes clay *firm and strong.*

object of a preposition   See *prepositional phrase.*

participial phrase   A present or past participle and its objects, complements, or modifiers. A participial phrase always functions as an adjective describing a noun or pronoun. Usually it appears immediately before or after the word it modifies: *Being a weight-bearing joint,* the knee is often injured. Plants *kept in moist soil* will thrive.

participle, past   A verb form usually ending in *-d, -ed, -n, -en,* or *-t: asked, stolen, fought.* Past participles are used with helping verbs to form perfect tenses (had *spoken*) and the passive voice (were *required*). They are also used as adjectives (the *stolen* car).

participle, present   A verb form ending in *-ing.* Present participles are used with helping verbs in progressive forms (is *rising,* has been *walking*). They are also used as adjectives (the *rising* tide).

parts of speech   A system for classifying words. Many words can function as more than one part of speech. See *adjective, adverb, conjunction, interjection, noun, preposition, pronoun, verb.*

passive voice   See *active vs. passive voice.*

personal pronoun   One of the following pronouns, used to refer to a specific person or thing: *I, me, you, she, her, he, him, it, we, us, they, them.* After Julia won the award, *she* gave half of the prize money to a literacy program. See also *antecedent.*

phrase   A word group that lacks a subject, a verb, or both. Most phrases function within sentences as adjectives, as adverbs, or as nouns. See *absolute phrase; appositive; gerund phrase; infinitive phrase; participial phrase; prepositional phrase.*

possessive case   See section 34a.

possessive pronoun   A pronoun used to indicate ownership: *my, mine, your, yours, her, hers, his, its, our, ours, your, yours, their, theirs.* The guest made *his* own breakfast.

predicate   A verb and any objects, complements, and modifiers that go with it: The horses *exercise in the corral every day.*

preposition   A word placed before a noun or noun equivalent to form a phrase modifying another word in the sentence. The preposition indicates the relation between the noun (or noun equivalent) and the word the phrase modifies. The most common prepositions are *about, above, across, after, against, along, among, around, at, before, behind, below, beside, besides, between, beyond, by, down, during, except, for, from, in, inside, into, like, near, of, off, on, onto, out, outside, over, past, since, than, through, to, toward, under, unlike, until, up, with, within,* and *without.*

prepositional phrase   A phrase beginning with a preposition and ending with a noun or noun equivalent (called the *object of the preposition*). Most prepositional phrases function as adjectives or adverbs. Adjective phrases usually come right after the noun or pronoun they modify: The road *to the summit* was treacherous. Adverb phrases usually appear at the beginning or the end of the sentence: *To the hikers,* the brief shower was a welcome relief. The brief shower was a welcome relief *to the hikers.*

progressive verb forms   See pages 167 and 184–185.

pronoun   A word used in place of a noun. Usually the pronoun substitutes for a specific noun, known as the pronoun's *antecedent.* In the following example, *alarm* is the antecedent of the pronoun *it*: When the *alarm* rang, I reached over and turned *it* off. See also *demonstrative pronoun; indefinite pronoun; intensive or reflexive pronoun; interrogative pronoun; personal pronoun; possessive pronoun; relative pronoun.*

proper noun   See section 37a.

regular and irregular verbs   When a verb is regular, both the past tense and the past participle are formed by adding *-ed* or *-d* to the base form of the verb: *walk, walked, walked.* The past tense and past participle of irregular verbs are formed in a variety of other ways: *ride, rode, ridden; begin, began, begun; go, went, gone;* and so on. See also section 26a.

relative adverb   The word *when* or *where,* when used to introduce an adjective clause: The park *where* we had our picnic closes on October 1. See also *adjective clause.*

relative pronoun   One of the following words, when used to introduce an adjective clause: *who, whom, whose, which, that.* The writer *who* won the award refused to accept it.

sentence   A word group consisting of at least one independent clause. See also *complex sentence; compound sentence; compound-complex sentence; simple sentence.*

simple sentence   A sentence consisting of one independent clause and no subordinate clauses: Without a passport, Eva could not visit her parents in Poland.

subject   A word or word group that names who or what the sentence is about. In the following example, the complete subject (the simple subject and all of its modifiers) is italicized: *The devastating effects of famine* can last for many years. The simple subject is *effects*. See also *subject after verb*; *understood subject*.

subject after verb   Although the subject normally precedes the verb, sentences are sometimes inverted. In the following example, the subject *the sleepy child* comes after the verb *sat*: Under the table *sat the sleepy child*. When a sentence begins with the expletive *there* or *it*, the subject always follows the verb. See also *expletive*.

subject complement   A word or word group that follows a linking verb and either renames or describes the subject of the sentence. If the subject complement renames the subject, it is a noun or a noun equivalent: That signature may be *a forgery*. If it describes the subject, it is an adjective: Love is *blind*.

subjunctive mood   See section 26c.

subordinate clause   A word group containing a subject and a verb that cannot stand alone as a sentence. Subordinate clauses function within sentences as adjectives, adverbs, or nouns. They begin with subordinating conjunctions such as *although, because, if,* and *until* or with relative pronouns such as *who, which,* and *that*. See *adjective clause*; *adverb clause*; *independent clause*; *noun clause*.

subordinating conjunction   A word that introduces a subordinate clause and indicates the relation of the clause to the rest of the sentence. The most common subordinating conjunctions are *after, although, as, as if, because, before, even though, if, since, so that, than, that, though, unless, until, when, where, whether,* and *while*. Note: The relative pronouns *who, whom, whose, which,* and *that* also introduce subordinate clauses.

tenses   See section 26b.

transitive and intransitive verbs   Transitive verbs take direct objects, nouns, or noun equivalents that receive the action. In the following example, the transitive verb *wrote* takes the direct object *a story*: Each student *wrote* a story. Intransitive verbs do not take direct objects: The audience *laughed*. If any words follow an intransitive verb, they are adverbs or word groups functioning as adverbs: The audience *laughed at the talking parrot*.

understood subject   The subject *you* when it is understood but not actually present in the sentence. Understood subjects occur in sentences that issue commands or give advice: [*You*] Put your clothes in the hamper.

verb   A word that expresses action (*jump, think*) or being (*is, was*). A sentence's verb is composed of a main verb possibly preceded by one or more helping verbs: The band *practiced* every day. The report *was* not *completed* on schedule. Verbs have five forms: the base form, or dictionary form (*walk, ride*); the past-tense form (*walked, rode*); the past participle (*walked, ridden*); the present participle (*walking, riding*); and the *-s* form (*walks, rides*). See also *predicate*.

verbal phrase   See *gerund phrase; infinitive phrase; participial phrase*.

Index

Documentation Directories

Continued >

Charts and Lists for Quick Reference

List of Sample Pages from Student Papers

Revision Symbols

abbr	abbreviation **38**	" "	quotation marks **35**
add	add needed word **19**	.	period **36a**
adj/ adv	adjective or adverb **28**	?	question mark **36b**
agr	agreement **25, 27a**	!	exclamation point **36c**
appr	inappropriate language **24**	—	dash **36d**
art	article **31b**	( )	parentheses **36e**
awk	awkward	[ ]	brackets **36f**
cap	capital letter **37**	...	ellipsis mark **36g**
case	case **27c, 27d**	/	slash **36h**
cliché	cliché **24b**	*pass*	ineffective passive **17b**
cs	comma splice **30**	*pn agr*	pronoun agreement **27a**
dm	dangling modifier **22c**	*ref*	pronoun reference **27b**
-ed	-ed ending **26a**	*run-on*	run-on sentence **30**
ESL	English as a second language/ multilingual writers **31**	*-s*	-s ending on verb **25, 31a**
frag	sentence fragment **29**	*sexist*	sexist language **24d, 27a**
fs	fused sentence **30**	*shift*	confusing shift **20**
hyph	hyphen **42**	*sl*	slang **24c**
irreg	irregular verb **26a**	*sp*	misspelled word **41**
ital	italics **40**	*sv agr*	subject-verb agreement **25**
jarg	jargon **24a**	*t*	verb tense **26b**
lc	use lowercase letter **37**	*usage*	see glossary of usage
mix	mixed construction **21**	*v*	voice **17**
mm	misplaced modifier **22a–b, 22d**	*var*	sentence variety **23**
mood	mood **26c**	*vb*	problem with verb **26, 31a**
num	numbers **39**	*w*	wordy **16**
om	omitted word **19, 31c**	//	faulty parallelism **18**
p	punctuation	^	insert
⌃,	comma **32a–i**	x	obvious error
no ,	no comma **32j**	#	insert space
;	semicolon **33a**	⌒	close up space
:	colon **33b**		
⌄	apostrophe **34**		

Detailed Menu